CO-PARENTING WITH A NARCISSIST: 7 SELF-RULES TO STAY SANE

A Survivor's Story

By GRACE W. WROLDSON

Copyright © 2020 by Grace W. Wroldson. Updated 2022.
All rights reserved.

Except for use in any review, no part of this book may be reproduced in any form without written permission from the publisher and author. This includes photocopying and recording or in any information storage or retrieval system. The publisher and author assume no responsibility for errors or omissions.

This publication contains the ideas and opinions of its author and is sold with the understanding that neither the publisher, nor the author, is engaged in the rendering of any mental health professional services. Readers requiring professional assistance, crisis support, therapy, or advice should contact a qualified professional. Any liability, loss or risk—personal or otherwise—which is incurred as a consequence, either directly or indirectly of the use and application of the contents of this book, is specifically disclaimed.

ISBN: 979-8-657211-37-5

Contact: http://www.GraceWroldson.com
Grace.W.Wroldson@gmail.com

Synopsis

Stuck. After ending the relationship with my child's father, I found myself attempting the impossible—co-parenting with a narcissistic ex. I was a loving, caring, concerned mother, but I was: criticized, attacked, blamed, discredited, smeared, and devastated by my ex. While in my care, our child was thriving. I worked overtime to protect her from the narc's subtle abuse and neglect. I was her buffer.

Cold. Cruel. Calculating. Clever. Charming. Conniving.

When he failed at controlling me, he sought to use legal means and the court system to take sole possession of our child. For eight years, he tried every narcissistic tactic to destroy me beyond what every professional involved had ever seen. In a cruel twist, he projected all his awful behavior onto me and he was awarded full custody. After I lost legal custody (and 50% physical), my goal changed to survival. I would not give up on my child! Through many hours of reflection, mediation, and therapy, I laid out my priorities. I would do my best to stay healthy and sane, validate my reality, and use protection agencies to the fullest extent.

Supported. Stable. Strong. Sane. Serene. Smart.

To repair my life, I identified 7 guiding principles that I call "Self-Rules." This book is a survival guide for overcoming the seemingly impossible parenting dilemma. I share my powerful insights and first-hand experiences with you. My hope is that you will find validation, emotional support, and encouragement on your journey to become the best person and parent that you can be.

Testimonials

"I loved this book! I could relate to everything she has gone through. Very easy to read and hard to put down! She has other books as well and I suggest if you haven't read her books that you do so!! Very well written and helpful!"

"The guidance tips offered in this book resonated with me. As someone who has four children with a narcissist, it was helpful to remind myself of what is important, as well as, how to keep stable by reading the Self-Rules. Each Self-Rule is significant. My anxiety was so high during the marriage that it took some time after the divorce for it to lessen. These Self-Rule guidances resonated with me on how I stayed sane during my divorce and through the co-parenting for my kids."

"Learned so much about how I could get the right mindset to get through co-parenting with a narcissist and my court custody battle. Glad that there are others out there struggling too. I feel less alone in the battle."

"It feels so impossible to deal with my narcissistic ex - at times. There are always problems due to his selfishness, greed, neglect, laziness, and arrogance. I needed some encouragement to keep showing up as a mom because I don't want to deal with him. This book provided me with that and hope."

Also by Grace W. Wroldson
_____

So, You Love an Alcoholic?: Lessons for a Codependent

I Loved an Alcoholic But Hated the Drinking: 11 Essential Strategies to Survive Codependency and Live in Recovery With Self-Love

How-To Fight a Narcissist in Family Court and Win: Super-Smart Strategies for Success

Co-Parenting with a Sociopath: Survival and Sanity Guide

How To Survive a Custody Battle with a Narcissist: When the Family Courts Force You to Co-Parent

Get Grace's follow-up book!

Available on Amazon!

For my child,
And all the children of this dilemma.

For mothers in pain.

"If a victim fights back, the narcissist will often fight back until the narcissist's prey deeply fears standing up for herself."
—*Ugly Love,* Laura Charanza

Contents

Disclaimer	i
About Grace Wroldson	v
Update	vii
A Special Thanks to…	xiii
The Serenity Prayer	xv
The Sanity Prayer	xvii
Welcome to My Wisdom	1
My Injustice	11
Self-Rule #1	19
Switch Focus and Survive	
Self-Rule #2	31
Learn to Coexist	
Self-Rule #3	41
Learn to Live With the Wins	
Self-Rule #4	49
Keep the Focus On Love	
Self-Rule #5	57
Continue Healing	
Self-Rule #6	65
Do Each Thing As It Comes	
Self-Rule #7	73
Write and Share	
Bonus: Self-Rule #8	81
Stage a Comeback	
Letter to My Readers	87
Helpful Resources	89
More About the Author	93

Disclaimer

First of all, my author name is a pen name. I write in a pen name for the protection of all involved because I am aware that sometimes labels can be harmful. However, I have found that accurate labels and descriptive terms are extremely helpful in pinpointing the problem, as well as finding the coinciding correct solution.

This isn't your average co-parenting situation after a divorce or break-up. I use the term "narc" for this book to shorten the word narcissist. I did this for ease in writing; it is not meant to be derogatory. Although his whole experience happened to me on a personal level, I know that this is an impersonal issue. This type of thing happens with this type of person. I was involved, but the involvement is a typical situation with a child or children involved— with an atypical person. It was all abject terror for me. However, I am a survivor.

Second, you need to know that I am not an expert on narcissistic personality disorder. I am not a clinical professional. Most importantly, I am not a legal expert. I do not have any legal training. Furthermore, I am not even a parenting expert. What I am is a mother who found herself continually failing at co-parenting with an uncooperative, angry ex. It came to my awareness quite late in the game that my child's father—a man that I refused to marry over a fifteen-year relationship—turned out to, indeed, be a narcissist with sociopathic tendencies, not just a drinking habit that he continually denied.

The legal system that I refer to is the U.S. Court System of the family courts located in New England. If you are also in America, please be mindful that each state has different guidelines and general types of case rulings. I realize that the family court problems that I experienced may vary from state to state and county to county. I am sure it is different in different countries, as well. Remember that you must follow your own legal counsel and understand your own laws, rules, and restrictions for your specific court jurisdiction.

Also, since a judge presides over the cases here, each ruling follows a judge's style of interpreting the law. Even more so, each lawyer has a different way of representing their clients. While some lawyers work to be reasonable and avoid trials, others seek to keep the case going and extract maximum legal fees by not allowing meaningful mediation to take place and head into trials for the billable hourly fee. The circumstances are vast and many. I often call into question the ethicality of lawyers practicing in family courts. I believe that this is unethical and doesn't consider the children who are caught in a war, where the legal professionals actually fuel and fight. This will all depend on the lawyers you are dealing with. Each attorney not only has an angle and style, but they will also adopt a strategy and play a legal game.

Trigger Warning: Some of the facts of my story may be very upsetting to read. I caution you to know this before reading the details of my legal tragedy, or what may have happened to my young child in the care of her father. My goal is to turn my personal tragedy into triumph, or at the very least, to turn this into a teaching tool for other mothers in similar situations.

What ails us? Narcissistic Abuse Syndrome is real and presents a danger to us associated with a narcissist. Professional help is recommended, and is often required, to deal with this type of abuse and abuser. I encourage you to seek out the help that is safe for you. Remember your safety at all times.

Please know that my thoughts and opinions are strictly my own. Take what you like, and leave the rest. This book is meant to be helpful and to validate any of you who have already lost custody of your child to a narcissist. For those of you who are going through this legal battle, it may shed some light on what is happening. The best advice that I got from my second attorney was to be reasonable, at all times, because that is how a judge will view me. I always remember that my actions or inactions will be judged by a judge—who may or may not have been a mother. Whenever I didn't know what to do, I reasoned things out with my attorney and many mental health professionals to craft a response that was adequate and respectful.

NOTE: This was written with open-hearted transparency so that you could see my healing process at the "mind level." These ***8 Self-Rules*** can be suggestions for you. These things are what I told myself and what I would have told a best friend going through something similar. I hadn't attained the outcome that I wanted–yet, but I had to teach myself how to get to a place I hadn't reached. This is my story; I hope it helps. *

*Disclaimer: These are helpful tips based solely on the author's thoughts and opinions. The author is not a qualified mental health professional nor a crisis caseworker. She cannot give legal advice or appropriate counsel and is therefore not liable for any injury, harm, or damages in your case (or situation). Please follow your doctor's, therapist's, counselor's, and lawyer's advice, as well as your own good common sense and intuition based on your unique case—to see if these tips could be helpful. Child custody situations vary whereas some of these will not be applicable to your circumstance. Furthermore, court orders may dictate otherwise. Please use your own good judgment when reading or using this book. This is for personal self-help only. These were created from the author's own lived experience and not based on any laws or rules of the courts. This is copyright protected by the author and is not to be sold, distributed, or quoted without the author's written consent.

About Grace Wroldson

Grace Wroldson: Mother, Author, Survivor, Thriver, & Life Coach

Grace is an award-winning author of five self-help books available on Amazon. Through her books, Grace gives insight into coping with loving an alcoholic. Her newest books deliver essential survival strategies for co-parenting with a narcissist in a high-conflict custody battle.

Years of loving an alcoholic hindered Grace with heartbreak. She loved him 100 ways that didn't work. Finally, after enduring a fifteen-year relationship full of struggle and pain, she was able to grasp recovery for herself and break free of her toxic codependency. By sharing her strength and truth in her books, she helps women shift, change, heal, grow, learn, and transform. Her steps remind readers they have the power of choice, and inspires women to step into the "self-love solution" and love themselves in and/or out of this dilemma—towards health, wellness, sanity, and freedom. Grace's lessons have helped women break what she calls the "codependent spell," unlocking confusion and conveying the truth that knowledge is power and freedom is the gift we give ourselves.

After that toxic relationship ended, Grace bravely fought on the "front lines" of family court for over ten years for custody and the safety of her child. By being a loving mother and advocating for her child, she was falsely accused, smeared, attacked, and scapegoated. Gradually, she came to realize that her ex was not just an alcoholic but also a narcissist. During the battle, Grace achieved various layers and levels of protection for her child. Sharing her real-life, first-hand experiences have helped many other mothers not feel so alone. She openly gives her hard-won tips, tools, and strategies for those who are forced to co-parent with a narcissist or sociopath. She shares how she recovered from losses and staged a comeback in her books. By offering her knowledge base, she encourages desperate mothers to "hang in there," revealing that almost all bad situations and court rulings can be turned around (or navigated) by using skillful-means and super-smart strategies.

Defying the odds, Grace overcame every obstacle that her ex placed in her path to happiness. She has since dedicated her life's work to helping other women and mothers cope, win, face failures, and find peace. Ultimately, her mission is to spare children from an alcoholic home and save them from abusive, toxic, personality-disordered parents by offering the secrets to her success and valuable survivor wisdom in her books, reminding mothers that they do have rights. So, follow her to the shores of sanity to learn, heal, and grow—with Grace.

Visit her at: www.GraceWroldson.com
Follow Grace on: Goodreads, Facebook, Twitter, Instagram, LinkedIn

Update 2022:

    I would like to thank all my readers for reading my books and bearing witness to my story. It was quite the saga! I moved from victim to survivor, then to thriver within the span of two years. What I can say is don't get lost in the pain; push through to get to the other side. It's truly worth it. One key to overcoming this pain quickly is to put it into perspective and realize this has happened to many a good mother.

    After writing 3 true-story books, and an ugly eleven-year family court battle over the custody of our child, I was finally able to establish peace with the narcissist. How did I do this? Well, it took strategy, planning, and follow-through. I had to use skillful means, be extremely patient, eliminate my weaknesses, and figure out what wins in family court. First, I had to establish a winning mindset and overcome my losses. That's what you will read about in this book. Mindset can be everything sometimes! If you are struggling, know that you are not alone. If you are in a custody battle and forced to co-parent with a narcissist, you will be placed in a predicament loaded with inherent problems. Be sure to get your mind clear, sane, and established firmly with your "Why" you are enduring this hell. NOTE: The chapter headings are the Self-Rules that I set that got me through the first leg of my battle. I battled for my sanity in the midst of insanity. Keeping my sanity saved my case and my child. Be smart, establish some rules.

    After losing my legal rights to my only child and sorting out my dilemmas, I was able to hire a more competent attorney and have the courage to file many contempts on my ex for non-compliance of the court order. I was able to win my rights back slowly and have my ex pay my legal fees. My child regained her therapist and got more protection. I received regular child support without issue. The judge began denying and dismissing his many motions. Read about that in my second follow-up book, *How To Fight a Narcissist in Family Court and Win*. I left all the drama, trauma, and chaos behind and opted for strategies and planning.

    Was I able to get a 100% perfect co-parenting relationship? No. Was I able to turn the angry narcissists' mind from me being the target of blame to lawyers and the courts? Yes. Was he nicer to me when I adopted key survival strategies? Yes. Did our child benefit from my survival and all the new neutralizing strategies that I implemented? Absolutely. You can read about this in my third book, *Co-Parenting with a Sociopath: Survival and Sanity Guide*. Am I happy with what I was able to accomplish by having self-discipline and establishing rules of conduct for myself? Yes! Was I able to cultivate contentment, regardless of what the narcissist was or wasn't doing? Yes!!

If you are desperate for a better way, I hope you read all three of my books. I want this for you. Even more so, I want this for your innocent child caught in the middle. Please learn all you can from me and my story. I write my story so that you can glean the wisdom for yourself, as I can't give you legal advice. Each case can be so vastly different but eerily similar. You will have to take what resonates for you. I lost but not "too badly" compared to the many stories that moms share with me in my private coaching practice. Knowing what I was up against and the tricks that would be placed, I prevented parental alienation and safeguarded myself against many false claims. These narcissistic tactics are important to be aware of. I call this Co-Parenting Abuse, and it's infuriatingly unjust and sometimes hard to prove. Educating myself on typical narcissistic patterns allowed me to stay a few steps ahead which was key. I documented like a paralegal pro and was a formidable opponent to disinformation. Because I was able to learn and change my ways, I changed my custody case in my favor. I not only staged a comeback but also set a tone for an easier life for myself and my child. If you can learn, then you can change what's happening and the outcomes.

My child went on to win all her activities back too from my disgruntled, litigious ex. As planned, she was able to be emotionally supported and surrounded by the eyes of the court, other court professionals, her therapist, his parents, and mainly me. I slowly backed up into the "spotlight" of family court, which made a difference. While my new lawyer strategized how to win with his carefully planned "chip-away-at-it method", I worked on dismantling the "enemy image" of me in his mind repairing some goodwill that was lost in battle. I became cooperative, non-confrontational, friendly, and seemingly a non-threat. When I eliminated some of my haunting fears, I changed my legal method from solely "defense mode" to occasional "offense mode." I compiled contempts so that my cases were more solid. In this way, the family court became a threat to him. After years of using family court to hurt me, he decided not to go there. With the wisdom of how to play the game, I made sure that every time he went to court, it was costly and unpleasant, and taught him a lesson that consequences are expensive and embarrassing. This made all the difference.

After reading this book, be sure to keep establishing healthy mindsets and learn what it takes to win in family court and then create peace. I hope my story of trials, tears, and transformation brings you to better days and happier parenting. We can't always change what happened to us, but we can choose how to live it.

XO —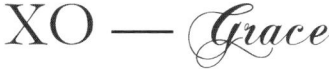

P.S. A note to all the fathers: Although I am a women's author and my mission is to help protective mothers, I want to shout out to the dads. I didn't expect so many fathers to read my books. Thank you if you are! I know many men with narcissistic exes who lose their money, health, children, and sanity to narcissistic mothers (who are just as bad as narcissistic fathers.) My heart goes out to you, too. It can be infuriating, confusing, and crazy. I know that you can be very concerned (rightly so) to have young children in the clutches of a narcissistic mother who often neglects and abuses children in ways that can be so subtle and hard/impossible to prove. Yet, we can see the damage to their precious little souls. Keep this in mind: While it may take only one high-conflict party to keep the conflict going in family court, it can take only one healthy, stable, solid parent to raise a healthy child. Be that healthy parent.

Here's my encouragement to the dads out there. Whether the storms. Opt-out of drama, trauma, and chaos. Stay away from any/all crazy-making behavior. Follow court orders. Focus on your child. Be the best dad you can be despite what your ex says about you. I believe that children can (and eventually do) make up their own minds based on being loved, your constant care and presence, and your actions. Be there when you can be. Make time. Do fun things with your child. Make memories that can't be erased. Don't get sucked into battles that draw your attention away from your child/children. Don't react. Before you respond, please "reason it out" with someone rational/civil/logical (or one of us experienced coaches who deals effectively with narcissists). Talk to a few trusted people to get a few perspectives to vent. (I find that tip to be the most helpful to my dad-friends who deal with the nonsense regularly.) When they talk to a few guy friends, they can calm down a bit. Don't be afraid or feel embarrassed to ask for help. Those who get the help, get the prize of peace and don't make mistakes that cost them in court. Also, in the long run, I have noted that dads tend to do better when a judge orders things versus caving and giving into a woman who constantly uses them. I have witnessed men get resentful and bitter after being used during and especially if it continues after the relationship. Don't allow that to happen to you. Don't get bitter, get better. It may be easier for you to accept the laws and rules (and calculations) over being taken advantage of repeatedly.

Also, don't hold it in. Get therapy to purge this pain and get the poison/toxin/pain/rage out. Your harboring resentments can come out sideways inadvertently, and the children feel it. Some children end up mistakenly blaming themselves. So, if your ex needs to experience the consequences of her behavior, allow it to happen; don't' enable her anymore. I understand it's hard to see someone get in trouble for bad behavior, but our children are counting on us. If you don't stand up to a narcissist, how will your child/children? Also, don't cave in to any false threats. Document them and keep detailed lists for evidence. Let the judge inform them what's up. Don't be the one who tries to deliver the voice of reason and ramifications. (Otherwise, you may be blamed.) Look for my book recommendations in the back of this book to continue your education. If you are reading this, I suggest you read those in addition.

Another word of wisdom for caring dads: please don't assume that you can represent yourself properly. I have seen many dads try to save money only to get emotional during their hearing or trial and then . . . lose their case. You need a lawyer who is a family court expert, not your tax attorney. Sometimes you will have to pay thousands to get the respect you have earned and are worth. Yes. It's part of the unfairness that we all have to face. But, you'll be amazed at how much nicer your ex can be when they have to "face the music" or your better lawyer, or a judge vs. control you through your fears and insecurities. Do what I had to do to turn my situation around. I shored up my weaknesses and become tougher with solid boundaries. Learn to say, "No" to your ex and prepare for the backlash, but stay firm. After all, we teach people how to treat us.

As you know, dads have rights too. I am in support of whoever is the protective, healthy, child-focused parent and non-abusive. I am sorry that you have to go through this too. Your children are lucky to have you. I always say that the only thing worse than a narcissistic father is a narcissistic mother. If you can, get your child/children into therapy ASAP - preferably from a narcissistic abuse expert. Because, often, regular therapists won't pick up on the mother being the issue. So, you need experts with experience who get it. Children will need to overcome shattered self-esteem, self-doubt, and other harmful effects of a narcissistic mother. But know that they can and do with support. Message me for names of great coaches that had narcissistic mothers and went on to thrive and become stronger than before. They now help others with what they went through. I personally know a few that have made it past the awful experience of a narcissistic mother who succeed in life despite what they went through in their childhood. Believe in yourself, and believe in your child.

If you can, push (even if you need a judge to order it - even if you have to pay extra) to have your children involved in sports, dance, scouts, and other events in the community. We aren't born with self-esteem, we have to build it. Self-esteem is our fundamental power. Be aware that a narc mother can stunt this growth for a child. I say: make a way, find a way. Then, go to these, even if you feel uncomfortable. Do so, even if you have to stand far away with a smile and a wave. Bring them a bottle of water, flowers, new batting gloves, whatever token helps them feel remembered, valued, and thought about. The more time they have building self-esteem and friendships, the better their chances are. And know that sometimes you have to take the lead in advocating for your children. Even if it has to go before a judge and become a court order because she doesn't have any decency. Children only get one childhood, don't allow the narcissist to ruin it completely. You can make a difference! Be sure to follow any court orders that restrict you, even if they are unfair. (Always find out your options. See if you can appeal with a better lawyer.) Allowing injustices to add up can really haunt us and lead us into depression. Fight against that. Use your anger constructively to build better boundaries and a better life for yourself and your child/children. I hope my words of encouragement help! Please feel welcome to read any and all of my books written to mothers and women. Learn all you can.

A Special Thanks to…

My dear friend, Pat, for saying out loud, "He's trying to control you! That's what this is about!"

I truly appreciated all your insight, truth, and support. You spent many hours listening to my fears, failures, and triumphs. With this book, I hope to rectify some of the personal hell that we have both lived through by exposing the abuse and injustice.

Thank you, especially, for coming to my first court appearance to witness just how badly the family judges do not understand alcoholism, or narcissistic abuse. Having you "in my corner" helped me endure the many more years of abuse by proxy. From the bottom of my heart, thank you! You were a godsend. Here's to hoping for a better future for mothers and justice for women and children.

The Serenity Prayer

A much-needed prayer for co-parenting with a narcissist.

The Serenity Prayer

God grant me the serenity to
Accept the things I cannot change
The courage to change the things I can
And the wisdom to know the difference.

—Reinhold Niebuhr

My Sanity Prayer

A much-needed prayer for dealing with narcissists in the legal system.

Dear Grace,
May I face with dignity the injustices,
and injuries that are inevitable in life.

May I gain courage through connection
with others to go forward fearlessly,
while maintaining reason, logic, common sense, and wisdom.

May I be able to discern what is worth using my energy for,
so that I can enjoy life
no matter what the insane person does or doesn't do.

And no matter what the outcome,
may I still believe in myself, and know the truth.

May my child always feel and know that they are loved.
May my care reach my child—even with the narcissist in the way.
Amen.

Welcome to My Wisdom

> "The only success I am having against the
> narc is personal success. I spoke up to him
> for the first time today! He didn't like it. I did."
> —*a journal entry*

Welcome to my story. I am here to revolutionize the way we women deal with narcissists. In this book of *7 Self-Rules*, I am here to share my secret recipe for success after a decade of failures. Just to be clear, the success I am referring to is personal success, not success against a narc. I will be redefining the word "win" throughout my story. My hope is that you make this major paradigm shift, too. Hopefully, my book empowers women. Injustice for one person is injustice for all of us.

> "I pray that love and justice will prevail. Even
> if the wheels of justice turn slowly."
> —*a journal entry*

The hard fact is that I could never make rules with the narc, nor successfully enforce them. I learned that a ruled-based approach with a narc is doomed to fail for several reasons. Once you understand how narcs generally operate, you can see why the objective to win against a narc is a losing battle. I found true success when I aimed to win the fights that were, 1) worth fighting for, and 2) winnable!

Setting up Self-Rules/Creating Principles to Live By

> "I loved a narcissist, but I wasn't loving myself!
> (Now, I must answer to this.)"
> —*a journal entry*

To win, I started to develop a simple set of rules with myself, and learned to stick with them. These ***Self-Rules*** were created from my own consciousness and derived from my morning meditations. I find that meditation is a very useful tool for gaining perspective, clarity, and peace. What I love about meditation is that you go inward for answers.

There was a point in my journey where I got tripped up by other people's opinions of my situation. I was handed so many strategies from other people, that I was severely confused and lacked direction of any kind. I discovered that I had to go inward for a formula that would work in my circumstance.

Over time, there were many great suggestions that I added to the mix, when appropriate. However, the best thing that I ever did for myself was to go inside, first, and find some peace. From a more peaceful state, I could then ask for simple answers. The second best thing that I did was set some rules for myself that I would follow going forward. To keep my eyes focused forward was a win!

The Narc and His Game

> **"It seems like everything is a game to him. He is dead-set on winning, no matter what it takes. My lawyer says that he is the type of person that would cut off his nose to spite his face! Ouch!"**
>
> —*a journal entry*

I discovered that narcs enjoy the game of destruction and will laugh the entire way through. I witnessed first-hand how he could carelessly cause trouble for himself and others, and I—to my shock and horror—realized that it strangely energized him. He thrived on drama. If you don't believe me because it sounds odd, well it is!

I encourage you to go research more about narcissistic personality disorder traits and come to a general/overall awareness of what they all have in common for traits, tactics, and motives. I learned that they are experts at trickery, since it is how they have had to survive their whole life. In this book, I want to show you whom I was able to change. And—*spoiler alert*—it wasn't the highly skilled narc… it was me!

> **"The name of the game for me is to stay alive! I need to survive this."**
>
> —*a journal entry*

How to Level the Playing Field

"I need to be smart enough not to self-sabotage."
—a journal entry

After playing the game in Family Court year, after year, attempting to protect our young child from his neglect and emotional harm, I learned a few lessons. One was how to level the playing field, as it seemed like the narc always had the upper hand with money and professionals willing to lie for him, not to mention his enabling, dysfunctional family who took the stand and lied for him, too. He rigged the entire game in his favor.

You see, good people don't want to see people get into trouble. We all rally to help. This is what a narc counts on, us good people who care. By using us, they can get their way, time and time again. It was up to me to smarten up and step out of my "good person" role into a brand new version of me. I did this gradually. It was an uncomfortable process, as it wasn't a skill I possessed yet. I began training to gain the muscles I would need to be an adequate match. I learned the very valuable skills of communicating and confronting.

My Secret Recipe for Success

It's no secret that my secret weapon against the narc was self-love. I would never share this with the narc. Only you! Over the years of being on the receiving end of his hate, I learned to love myself. I learned to respect myself, even if he couldn't. I honored my gut instincts and opinions, no matter how much he tried to make me feel wrong. Most importantly, I conquered my self-doubt. Once I did that, he lost a tremendous advantage over me.

I changed many more things to gain personal success. I changed how I related to others in the world by creating personal boundaries and practicing self-preservation. I vowed to self-protect my time, money, energy, and resources. I looked inward for healing, instead of outward, toward him, to help me feel whole. I changed at a fundamental level and came back to my core self. I completed several abuse recovery programs, and shored up all the wounded parts of me from childhood, allowing me to grow into an adult. I handled the triggers with maturity by seeking help from professionals. I kept a healthy lifestyle for myself, and learned to care for my needs, and, through this, my child benefited from all that I did to help myself.

"She looks to me. So, I have to be healthy."
—a journal entry

Even more so, I decided to only ask for help from the experts on narcissism. I stuck to my principles of playing a fair and honest game. I stopped giving in to his bullying, and I stopped caring about what he thought, or said about me. I stopped taking advice from well-meaning friends, because they were trying to apply logic to my situation, and most of the time, that never seemed to work with a narc.

> **"I will never again care what a person who lacks empathy and compassion for others, thinks of me!"**
> *—a journal entry*

Personal Growth is Where "It's" At!

When I met my biggest despair of losing legal custody of my 8- year-old daughter to my ex, the narc, I cried for months. My support groups, therapists, and counselors felt as helpless as I did. They couldn't help me. Nothing they said mattered at that time, because I felt like I had lost the battle for the most valuable thing in my life. Even though I had researched the topic of narcs and court, and even though I had followed all the advice to do the right thing, I was no match for a professional liar willing to stoop extremely low to win. The narc was inhumane.

This time around in Family Court, I lost half-physical custody. And I say "this time," because we had been in court for her entire life. There were many court contempts, motions, agreements, filings, and finally, a lengthy trial. Everything the narc could throw at me, he did, and I was bruised and battered emotionally by it all. My character was called into question—something that I highly valued.

When it felt like there was nothing I could do, I started to go on long walks with my pain, sometimes for two full hours until I'd sit down somewhere in nature, asking God, "Why!?" I didn't know who to talk to, or blame, so I decided that God would be it. Friends and family weren't there for me. Instead, they hung up on me when I started yelling and crying that no one was helping me pay for a better lawyer, or testifying on my behalf. I was broken and brokenhearted. The pain was so excruciating at times, and the fear I suffered through, was gut-wrenching.

> **"The narc is not human. How can you enjoy taking a child away from their mother?"**
> *—a journal entry*

On top of that, I felt humiliated. I was an upstanding citizen of my small community. I subbed as a teacher's assistant in my daughter's elementary school, and I was a member of the PTG. How could I face everyone and tell them that I had lost custody of my child? The embarrassment was more than I could bear in my small town. Friends knew what I was going through, and to "save face," I warned them that I might lose the trial. Every single member of his family was on his witness list, and I felt like no match against his enabling, wealthy family.

Meditation Solution

To clear my mind, I started meditating. It was a practice of clearing the mind and not attaching to any thoughts. I was so sick of being in the mental space of fear, anger, rage, and worrying about how to fix it, and what to do, that I was mentally and emotionally exhausted. The long walks helped move all the pent-up energy around, while the sitting meditations in nature brought me back to balance and stillness. That's when I started to get some answers from the Universe. Before immersing myself in this daily practice, I was too blocked and clogged with emotions to let anything "in" until I processed all my pain. The meditations proved to be life-saving and valuable beyond measure.

Here is a list of the answers that I obtained from those long walks and deep meditations, in the order that I received them:

#1. Survive

My first answer after the brutal loss was: "survive." It felt like I was told by a power greater than myself to just survive. Though this message seemed to come from outside of myself, there was a still, small voice within that agreed. It was wise and basic advice, but I needed to hear it just the same. From that clear answer—from that turning point—I started to focus on eating, sleeping, breathing, living, running my household, maintaining my car, paying bills, and anything to do with basic survival in 2020. It was practicing "first thing's first." I was taking it one day at a time with the purpose of staying alive. Sometimes it felt hard to do. Somedays I couldn't get out of bed, but I knew that I had to feed and water myself. It was a type of at-home self-rehabilitation. I felt like a wounded animal with a broken wing. I needed some convalescent time.

#2. Learn to Coexist

My second survival answer was: "learn to coexist." I did not like this one, because it implied that the narc was still going to be around, and possibly, in power for the duration of my and my child's life. It was a horrifically scary thought. I was rendered temporarily powerless to seek justice with the corrupt legal system and lying lawyers. However, in accepting this answer to "coexist," I knew that the best I could do for now was to live with the problem and learn to do it well. This meant attaining a new level of acceptance of a life that was not as I imagined. Life isn't fair. Period.

#3. Live with the Wins

In my third meditation, I received the guidance of: "learn to live with the wins." I learned to rejoice in the truth that, despite the judge ordering the narc to have sole legal and half-physical custody, he took the time to carefully write a thirty-four-page judgment with many interventions that protected our child and allowed her rights. So, even though I lost a lot of rights, my child and I gained some important conditions, too.

For example, she was allowed to have a regular, consistent schedule, which is good for children, and good for me to plan my life and work around. She was allowed phone calls to me on certain days, at certain times, something the narc never allowed before. I was awarded more child support, which was not something I had asked for, at all.

We were ordered into co-parenting therapy to discuss our ongoing issues, which he would never agree to before, no matter how many times I asked to work things out with a mediator. He was ordered to log into Our Family Wizard (OFW), daily, and do meaningful co-parenting, which was another thing he never did before.

Prior to this new order, the narc had only used the co-parenting, court-ordered email portal, Our Family Wizard, for angry rants, finger-pointing, and abuse. All of these new provisions could be considered little wins under the giant loss.

#4. Focus on Love

> **"Living with the narc's dysfunction, I tend to lose myself."**
> —*a journal entry*

My fourth meditation message was to: "focus on love." I needed to make love my primary focus in life. It was too much for me to constantly be focused on how much I hated him and hated what he had done to me, so I needed to get back to the things that I loved. I was so sick of being consumed by hate. I needed the healing vibration of love to permeate my mind, body, and spirit, and most importantly, I had to focus on how much I loved my child and our time together. I had to shift my perspective, and see my situation from a higher angle. This higher angle was to see my dilemma symbolically, and to draw analogies from nature. I used metaphors to attempt to understand my situation with the narc.

> **"I have to nurture what I love to do and immerse myself in it; otherwise, the narc steals the love and joy right out of my life."**
> —*a journal entry*

#5. Keep Healing

> **"I will do anything now to protect my serenity after having it stolen for two decades."**
> —*a journal entry*

The fifth message from meditation was: "keep healing." The trauma from everything the narc dished out daily was painful and triggering. Even though I had done many recovery programs, I still had more healing work to do, so I had to continue my healing journey and keep up-leveling myself. Basically, I had to grow into a more healed person of high integrity who is strong and courageous in the face of adversity, and not easily triggered, while maintaining my reason, logic, and good judgment. Mostly, I needed to request fairness. While healing from a broken person to a whole person, I was learning how to be fair to myself, because the narc wouldn't be, nor would his lawyer.

What did healing mean?

It meant so many things to me: anything from traveling, completing degree programs, living where I always wanted, changing jobs, letting go of toxic friends, getting massages, writing, volunteer work, having a daily gratitude practice, learning about healing, reading books for pleasure, and more. I believe that healing is a personal recipe, and the recipe needs different ingredients, depending on the individual traumas. In all my studies of how we heal, I believe that the individual recipe for healing has to bake in the subconscious mind, and be thoroughly cooked to completion. Healing is a process. I think truth is the main ingredient.

> **"Trauma is like housework: it isn't going anywhere."**
> —*Melanie Tonia Evans*

#6 Do Each Thing as it Comes

The sixth message was an answer to my continual fears that kept popping up. I got the grounding advice to: "do each thing as it comes." This was an answer to the reality that the narc wasn't done causing problems parenting—that he was inherently disordered, and would keep making a mess of things. Before this new judgment, I would try to prevent things and be proactive, always trying to anticipate his next move. That strategy was exhausting for me. I needed to have a better plan that wasn't continually putting me in fearful mental projections, because living that way was so difficult. It was 100% fear-based living, and it wasn't healthy for me, or my child. I was in perpetual reaction-mode and lost my ability to respond logically at times. I also had to NOT make mountains out of molehills. I had to use every single tool from every recovery program on the new problems that cropped up, and sharpen my skills. Knowing that I was dealing with a narc, and educating myself, provided a level of immunity for me since he couldn't infiltrate my mind anymore. The only thing he had left was using the courts to attempt to gain power over me. I discovered that this tactic is called abuse by proxy. I survived it first-hand.

"I have to put my recovery program to work, so it can work."
—*a journal entry*

#7. Write

The seventh message was to: "write." So, I began journaling my story and my coinciding recovery. I began writing down my truths as they came. This was very validating for me. It was like having a best friend to talk to who knew the extent of the problem with the narc. I wasn't sure that anyone wanted to hear about my awful story, or that it would be helpful, but then, one day, I heard about a mother who ended up having supervised visitation with her daughter due to the narc's successful legal campaign—something my ex was after, too. It was then that I realized I was on the right track with writing, and if I could at least validate one other mother, it would have helped the world be a more friendly place for those mothers' experiencing similar pain and tragedy. So, whatever needed to come out onto the page, I let it. I had to write through my healing journey. Writing helped me cement my scattered thoughts.

"I think I am writing to heal myself from what just happened."
—*a journal entry*

Bonus #8. Stage a Comeback

> *"The best I could get at controlling him was to control my fears. And use the courts."*
> —*a journal entry*

Once I had a firm grasp of myself, my last and final message of hope was to: "stage a come-back." I knew that it was going to take time and diligence, but I had decided to never give up on my child. I would need to persevere. I needed to practice endurance. I had to be resilient. I had to be patient while practicing good principles of living. I needed to hire a better attorney, take wise counsel, be productive, and wait for my next day in court. I was determined to stop playing defense and, no matter how scary it felt, start playing offense with a new legal strategy. I was willing to heal, grow, and have the courage to change. Even more so, I was becoming brave enough to confront.

I was also willing to read more books, learn more on the topic, educate myself on family law with self-help programs, and consult more attorneys. I was willing to follow the advice from my meditations to survive, coexist, live with the wins, focus on love, keep healing, and do each thing as it comes. I was even brave enough to write, even while feeling utterly humiliated. I was daring to act boldly and to have the audacity to stage a comeback. I think that when a mother like me is stripped of her dignity and rights, and when there isn't much else to lose, a type of titanium backbone gets established, and the hero mechanism is launched. I found my journey to be a mother's hero journey.

> *"If you always do what you've always done, you'll always get what you've always got."*
> —*Henry Ford*

Are you stuck too?

If you are stuck in a similar situation, it may be beneficial to not only get into a narcissistic abuse recovery program and private individual therapy, but also to prioritize walking, meditation, prayer, and writing. I found this plan of self-therapy helpful to endure the Family Court battles since there seemed to be no end in sight, and only the court could accomplish things with a narc. I was never able to get the narc to cooperate out of the goodness of his heart. He lacked the ability. He only added stress.

> **"Women/mothers need emotional support
> for the horrible stress of this situation."**
> —*a journal entry*

    The disclaimer of this book is that what worked for me, may not work for you. So many of these situations are sticky and loaded with complicated legal matters. So please, take what you like, and leave the rest. I am not an expert on narcissistic personality disorder, nor do I have a degree in psychology. What I offer is my experience, strength, and hope. My wish for you, is that you find something useful that helps you and your child have a better life, despite the narc. When the focus is on yourself, and living a happy life with dignity, I believe you win.

My Injustice

> **"There is NO fairness for me to be gained with (or from) the narc. I must accept this."**
> —*a journal entry*

Whenever I was dealing with the narc, there was never any fairness available for me. This was a solid truth. As a matter of fact, the narc never even attempted—nor tried—to be fair to me. The selfish, self-centered nature of the disorder is that way because it truly has a blind spot. A narc can't see another person's needs. I had to come to terms with the outcomes of expecting fairness and put those expectations to bed. What I wasn't expecting was a corrupt court system and a legal game that was rigged to favor the wealthy, and not the truth.

> **"I can no longer expect fair treatment by the courts. Also—I can no longer expect that the courts can detect a narc at work."**
> —*a journal entry*

It's no secret that I suffered from injustice in the Family Court system. The court system was unable to detect a narc at work, in his game. This also means that my child suffered by having to spend more alone time with him, and even felt like she was a hostage, at times. She was afraid of her father, and rightly so. However, he had a tendency to buy puppies at just the right time, and large expensive toys to offset the lack of emotional safety, but it never truly worked.

Along with that sad reality, Child Protective Services also failed us on many occasions. They failed to investigate the deception and web of lies of the narc, and uncover just what was happening to my young daughter in various horrendous incidents. It is every mother's worst nightmare scenario. Feeling defeated, I took to documenting the drama, since it felt like the only thing that I could do. I began praying and attempting to find another way to keep my child safe.

> "I need to start being fair to myself. Because he doesn't have fairness to offer me—ever. Period."
> —*a journal entry*

Historical Injustices

I knew that I wasn't the first woman to lose legally to a narc. We have domestic violence shelters and agencies for a reason. It took time to get those established, and there had to have been a great need and a widespread problem. I was surprised by a famous story of a woman in England in the 1800s, Caroline Norton, who left her abusive, alcoholic husband and three sons, to save her life and to write. She had escaped the abuse, heartbreakingly left all her possessions and her children, just to survive. She took refuge in a friend's house and began writing her story for the local papers and gaining support for court.

> "How can I lose my child to a father that neglects her? I care for all her needs. I do everything for her. He can't/won't/doesn't care. I even volunteer at her school, organize the PTG Arts and Enrichment program, and sub as a paraprofessional there. Over the times he has had her, she suffered a serious head injury, frostbitten toes, bug bites all over her body, and a tick that was carrying two forms of Lyme Disease! And still, her father was awarded custody??? I don't get it.
>
> AND . . . How does a loving mother lose custody when she reports to child protection agencies that her young daughter has two urinary tract infections, and the child actually tells both therapists that her father and uncle are touching and treating her inappropriately? This . . . all while she's sleeping at the uncle's house that is not certified for occupancy yet? How, God? How!? Someone needs to tell me how this happens! Every system has failed her! Lord, have mercy on me."
> —*a journal entry*

Lady Caroline Norton lost in court. I can imagine the depths of the mother's pain. The injustice is infuriating. She originally couldn't get a divorce, nor ever see her children for a second. To add insult to injury, her husband took her profits from writing and sent her boys away so that she could definitely never see them. It doesn't stop there. To make matters worse for her, he further accused her of adultery with the Prime Minister and had them both put on trial. Her narrow escape and tragic legal drama was exactly the type of thing a narcissist does. It's classic retaliatory behavior. It is shocking to hear, by today's standards, that a woman was unable to obtain a divorce and was denied access to her three children; however, it sounded strangely familiar to me. I also left the narc, and that's not a choice you make lightly due to the fear of the ramifications and retaliations. These have happened throughout history—as they did me.

What that woman had to do in order to get a divorce and win rights for women was unimaginable at that time. She had to speak out. She had to go against white male authority. She had to leave behind everything, and even abandon her own children. Today, I take for granted that I could just easily break up with him, on my terms, when in her day, just two hundred years ago, a woman couldn't. I started to compare my situation to what it was like back then and realize just how much I had to be grateful for. I had rights that she never had, even though the narc still played all the same "I will get control of you" cards in an attempt to crush a woman's spirit. She was a brave soul to have endured the injustices of the day. She was a true hero for mothers' rights, because her work and story laid a foundation for the society to build something better. We needed some safeguards and rights. I began to see just how important it was to tell my story.

How do I deal with the injustice?

> **"After talking with the new attorney, I have realized that I have rights that I didn't even know I had. The only problem is, how do I exercise them with a narc who doesn't think I have any, or should have any? And how angry will he get to see me exercise them?"**
> *a journal entry*

At first, after the judge's order, I wanted to curl up into a ball in bed and just die. It certainly felt like death. The injury of having my rights removed cut deep into my DNA, and my trust in goodness was lost. I feared for my child's safety anytime she was unsupervised with the narc, her own father. It was the courts that awarded this, as I would have never allowed unsupervised time. Even the child protection agencies allowed this by closing cases and "unsupporting" the allegations. On top of that, his high-powered attorney used every clever legal tactic to get him sole legal custody and allowed this injustice by being his unethical accomplice. It was the complete opposite of what needed to happen for our child to be safe, physically, mentally, and emotionally.

> **"I know that failure just simply means I tried, but I feel like a failure as a mother. I know there is a difference."**
> —*a journal entry*

Initially, I had major doubts about whether I should even write this book. I felt unqualified and unhappy with my situation. I wondered if hearing my story, and the advice I gave to myself to get through the process of Family Court and raising a child with a narc, would help anyone. I wasn't an expert on narcissism, by any means. I barely understood the disorder. Was I wasting my time going over my traumatic story? Would my book even matter? I had the urge to create something good from my negative experience, as well as listen to the guidance that was within.

My bout of self-doubt lingered for a year. My anger was directed at everyone, including myself. I became frustrated with my life and started to complain about it. I was never hoping to be a writer. I never wanted any of it on my plate, because I had other dreams and aspirations. Instead, I found myself writing about injustice, suffering abuse by proxy at the hands of a narc, and it made me so discouraged. Was I just telling my horror story because I had lost power, and writing it down was the only thing I could do for the time being? Who would want to hear my horror when they were living their own with the many different types of narcs out there?

> **"The narc problem can't be solved, just coped with."**
> —*a journal entry*

The #1 Superpower Against a Narc

The good thing was that I didn't doubt myself when it came to him, the narc. The superpower that I developed was self-trust. Friends living with covert narcs encouraged me to continue writing, as they thought it was a great book for me to write. They reminded me of just how much personal experience I had on the topic, and that my experience could potentially help so many mothers. They advised me to be real—to tell the good and the bad—and not just write about the helpful lessons that I've learned. They recommended that I include the bad stuff, especially the many, many setbacks. They thought that my readers would find me believable when I was real. They also told me that reading my drafts was helping them already, because they felt less alone.

> **"My freedom from the narc is a real and true power."**
> *—a journal entry*

I appreciated the feedback, because I was experiencing setbacks every other day with the likes of a narc. It was the nature of the beast. I had my suspicions that my situation was worse than most, simply because I broke up with the narc—"on my terms." I had healed enough to finally call, "Enough!" with the narc. Because of the shot to the narc's ego, the type of treatment that I was used to getting from the narc—the passive-aggressive, subtle finger-pointing—had turned up a level. He changed how he treated me once I was no longer under his control, and I got the more horrible side of narcissism, from that point on.

Basically, I got the treatment of how he treated other people that he had contempt for. I know that the women who were married to narcs were paying attention to that detail of my story, because they, too, suspected that, as soon as they stood up for themselves, the narc would stand against them. And it certainly was something to be concerned about, knowing the narc's character and capabilities! I found that the reason that most women stay with the narc is due to the fact that they are attempting to safely raise young children. They are smart, yet scared, women who can foreshadow the consequences of pissing off a narc and leaving to go practice self-love and self-respect.

> **"My lawyer said that this order is just temporary. At the bottom of the thirty-four-page order, it says, "until further orders of the court."**
> *—a journal entry*

How to heal?

What felt like a true injury to me was the Family Court system being convinced that I was the terrible mother that the narc claimed I was, and stripping me of my legal rights. When researching how to heal from the unfavorable legal outcome, I learned more about the other side of injustice—how to live with it in the aftermath. I learned that injustice had to be acknowledged for me to heal. Otherwise, it would just hang over my head and weigh me down mentally, physically, and spiritually.

> **"People need to know what happened to me."**
> *—a journal entry*

To heal, I needed my total unfairness to be witnessed and validated by another compassionate person. I needed someone to listen to my story. I needed an emotional scribe to document what had happened, and acknowledge that it was unjust. I need it acknowledged that my dignity as a good, loving, caring mother was violated. When I discovered this wisdom—that to heal I needed acknowledgment—it felt right to me. I knew instinctively that this would be how I could heal for real, and not just carry the pain around in silence with me. Since there were no experts on narcissism in my area, and I didn't have the money to pay for a better attorney, I decided to write, myself—for myself.

> **"What happened to me was unfair."**
> *—a journal entry*

A Return to Power

I learned that there was one more important thing that had to happen to put completion and closure on my trauma of injustice. It had to be undone. I had to empower another person. There is a type of freedom in being empowered. I knew how I had lost power, and if I could warn others about the pitfalls and traps of dealing with a narc, I might be able to save at least one other mother and child. Some spiritual teachers I consulted talked about how you could heal injustice through some greater act of fairness to another. I made it my mission to find a way to do this.

> **"I do not want to preoccupy myself with an enemy.
> That's just another self-inflicted injustice."**
> *—a journal entry*

To get to the core of my dilemma, I had to reflect on matters of power. Power was the #1 thing that the narc was after. It was what was stolen from me in Family Court in terms of parenting. I was stripped of my power to make decisions for my child by losing legal rights. However, I held the power to petition, the power to file complaints, the power to speak up, the power to confront, and other powers that I wasn't comfortable using. Losing power in one setting forced me to access those other powers that I wasn't used to enacting. I knew that the uncomfortable nature of going to those alternative forms of power was my "growth edge." In order for me to step into my power, I would have to grow.

> **"Even if I am unsuccessful in regaining my legal rights back
> in Family Court, I will have successfully told my story."**
> *—a journal entry*

The Nature of Growth

The nature of growth hit me one day on my regular walk. I sat down and picked at the grass with my restlessness. Mindlessly, I picked up a helicopter seed and studied it. I knew that it held the potential of being a mighty maple tree someday. All the little thing needed was to be placed in the darkness and given the right ingredients for growth. It needed room to grow, safety, water, sunlight, air . . . it needed all the things that I, too, needed for my growth. I was inspired by nature's process, diligence, and potential.

> **"I had so much potential before the destructive, soul-sucking relationship with the narc. I wonder if it's still there? Am I still there?"**
> —*a journal entry*

Holding onto that seed was more than just symbolic for me. I felt like I was holding onto a seed inside of myself. It was giving me a type of supernatural strength. I looked up at the sky and started to imagine that I, too, was holding potential in my shell. That someday, I, too, could be like one of the mighty maple trees towering over my head, enduring the storms of life and still standing brilliantly strong.

It was amazing to hold that tiny seed in my hand while looking at the full version of the maple tree in front of me. What contrast! This small thing that was let go, only to fall off to the ground, was loaded with great big potential. It had the DNA of becoming. It had the code of something grand, locked in its core make-up. It just simply needed to grow.

> **"I need to grow through this experience, not just go through it."**
> —*a journal entry*

Becoming and growing needed my time and attention. To accomplish my purpose, I had to be a constant gardener. The maple seedling would have to survive, endure, be resilient, and patiently make its way upward to the sky. First, it had to root down deep into the earth to make the journey upward. Then for protection, it had to cover its stem with thick bark. Finally, no matter the weather or circumstances, it would have to reach up higher, and open its leaves to the sunlight. It had to expand and evolve. It had to be what it was about to become.

> **"My way through this is through myself."**
> —*a journal entry*

I felt all those similar desires stirring in me. I needed to get firmer roots in my life, financially and legally, and I needed to protect myself with a stronger shield of covering, learned from the narcissism experts. Mostly, I had to grow tougher skin to endure the abuse. Finally, to flourish, I would need to open up and breathe in the fresh air and new wisdom to reach new levels of growth and become all that I was meant to be. I, too, needed years—maybe even decades—of growth to reach my true potential as a person. I needed to withstand all the winds, fires, and flying objects in my life.

> **"Am I willing to face more prosecution in the name of truth and justice? Because going forward would expose me to more narcissistic abuse. Is there any way to become immune to it?"**
> —*a journal entry*

To remind me daily, and symbolize my potential, I took that seed home in my pocket. Before I left, I planted another one so that I could watch it grow weekly and remind myself that sometimes it takes long years to grow strong, and into what I am meant to be. The seed became a seedling, and I felt a sense of hope watching it grow leaves. I watched myself grow, too.

> **"I have greatness locked up inside of me.
> I have the potential to grow."**
> —*a journal entry*

Suggestion: Establish a Healthy Mindset for Dealing with Injustice (Learn to accept that bad things can happen to good people. And understand (if you are discouraged and shocked) that unfairness has happened over the entire history of humanity. Yet, we advance, implement new laws, and evolve past the unfairness, and work to make the world a better place. Learn to hang on if your judge and circumstances aren't there yet. Know that you are not alone in this problem.)

Self-Reflection Questions:

- What is your story of injustice?
- In what ways were you harmed?
- What parts of co-parenting have been unfair to you?
- Is there anything that can be done using the laws, letters, or petitions?

Self-Rule #1

SWITCH FOCUS AND SURVIVE

Math Equations, Mantras, and Mothering Stop Focusing on What Can't Be Fixed = The Narc

Focus on Coming Back to Self = Healing

> **"To survive is to win."**
> —*a journal entry*

Before my narcissistic abuse recovery started helping me heal, every minute, of every hour, of every day I was focused on the narc—all to my own detriment. I obsessed over what he was and wasn't doing. I was so focused on him, that I barely saw myself. Unfortunately, I was mistakenly focusing on something that couldn't be fixed, or more accurately, I was focusing on someone who couldn't be fixed. It was my daily dilemma, and I saw no easy way out. I was merely surviving his abuse tactics and trying to keep our child alive. At times, it was absolutely terrifying to try to co-parent with the narc. It felt like swimming in shark-infested waters whenever I got into an argument or court battle with him. Sometimes, I was so tired of dealing with him, all I could do was merely float, but, for my child, I had to survive.

> **"I need to adopt a winning mindset. As long as she has me as a mother, she is not at a disadvantage. I repeat: To survive is to win."**
> —*a journal entry*

1a. Reframe Everything as a "Win"

> **"My therapist assured me that when I change the way I look at things, the things I look at will change."**
> —*a journal entry*

    The bottom line was that I recognized that my survival was everything for her. After one particular legal battle, I felt like I had lost so much. Other battles hadn't been so bad, but when I shared that acknowledgment of my loss with a friend, he pointed out to me all my wins. He suggested that I balance out my so-called "losses" with whole picture thinking. My friend reminded me to balance things out in my mind if I got stuck on ruminating about something that I was classifying as a loss. He assured me that I was having many "wins" and small victories along the way, even though I lost a huge custody battle. To fix my mind and help generate better thinking, I began reframing everything in terms of my "wins," and that's where I started to put my focus.

> **"I need to practice the tool of reframing my losses, seeing the big picture, and focusing on my 'wins.'"**
> —*a journal entry*

    I was able to recognize one gift in losing half of the custody time with my daughter in Family Court. When the narc had his parenting time, I had just enough time to be with myself and attempt to see what was happening to me. I finally had the opportunity to come back to myself, to honor myself, and to do the self-care I needed.

> **"I have to stop programming myself to think that I lost. My therapist says that I have to stop telling my brain that."**
> —*a journal entry*

    When dealing with the narc, I was tired, broke, in weekly therapy, drained, taking responsibility for all his messes, putting up with excessive use of court tactics, forced to try co-parenting classes, facing the daily word battles on Our Family Wizard, and more. Even my close, confidant friends, therapists, and loving church community were exhausted from hearing my tales of woe. I was surviving the devastation of repeatedly "losing" in Family Court and losing my mind. My mental health was always at risk when dealing with the narc.

"To think of myself and not him is to win in each moment."
—a journal entry

The only time that I felt any semblance of feeling good was when I was by myself and just thinking of me. It was amazing how peaceful and serene it was just to be by myself for days after he won half-physical custody. I thought the void from being without my primary job of being a mom would devastate me. I thought I would die from fear, anxiety, and worry, but what actually happened was I got to enjoy a much-needed "mommy-break." It was like I got a chance to come up for air in a war where smoke bombs were being thrown at me daily.

On one long walk, ruminating about his latest "word salad" on Our Family Wizard, I realized that all his snarky co-parenting remarks on OFW were just him "blowing smoke." His words were like stinky smoke bombs used to disorient and confuse me. When I realized how his words were just a desperate attempt to deflect and leave the scene, I gained a huge amount of hope, as I no longer had to worry about his words being true and harmful; they were simply smoke.

"To not be with the narc in a relationship is to win."
—a journal entry

When the new court order forced him to log in and use OFW, he complied—somewhat. He surely wasn't going to use that electronic communication tool for healthy conversation. Instead, it became an outlet for his anger and unhappiness. I became so weighed down by how fast he could "shoot from the hip," shooting a message back to me loaded with accusations, criticisms, and under-handed comments. It was like his brain was warped, but worked at warp speed, and in his mind, I could tell that I was his "enemy." Engaging with him cost me what I call: "vital life force energy." It was always a draining battle dealing with someone so disordered, fundamentally unhappy, and chronically angry. This awareness was immensely helpful to me.

"To not engage in battle is to win."
—a journal entry

Reflecting on why I became such a dumping station for his garbage, I learned that you don't leave a narc on your own terms without bruising his ego. From that point on, in order to preserve his ego, I had to be put down, undercut, and basically destroyed. His style was much like a bully with low self-esteem on a playground— where they only feel better by picking on someone else. I was that someone else. For eight long years, I was his target. Essentially, he lost control of me and had to up his game, and, yes, it was all a game to him.

> **"To no longer be controlled by the narc . . . is to win."**
> *—a journal entry*

1b. Do Your Math

When nothing added up with the narc, I came up with my own simple math equations for survival:

> **"Focus on the alcoholic narc = Lose precious life force energy. Focus on myself and heal = Gain Energy. Interesting to note."**
> *—a journal entry*

I noticed that on my days off from full-time parenting when I turned inward to heal, I became recharged. When I made my healing my primary focus, I made tremendous progress. I got my power back. Energy returned to my body so that I had the energy to live my life. I realized that if I wanted my power back after years of losing it to a narc, then I would have to spend an equivalent number of years pursuing personal healing. First of all, I needed space for my personal growth and healing, including a safe place and emotionally safe people. I also needed time-outs from life, and time away from him. The courts gave me that with the many interventions I won in previous rounds of Family Court. I needed poetry, music, compassionate friends, hobbies, long walks, candlelit bubble baths, good spiritual books, church sermons on YouTube, motivational TED talks—I needed all of it to heal on all levels.

Most importantly, I needed wisdom from the experts on narcissism. I needed to hear what was true. The whole ordeal was beyond my level of understanding and reasoning, but they explained the things that were happening to me on subtle, incomprehensible levels. I knew in simple terms that he wasn't acting right, but to put a label on it and know what tactics were being used against me gave me great reassurance and validation. Knowledge also became a source of my personal power.

> **"To stop trying to understand the narc is to win!**
> **To stop trying to justify his actions or make excuses for him . . . is to win."**
> *—a journal entry*

Dealing with the narc was like trying to type computer code into a computer when I had no idea how computers even worked. I would sit in front of the screen on OFW and type, type, type, trying to fix the corrupt program with more communication, only to have the hard drive spit out more corrupt code for everything in life. I never found the algorithm to make him function as a good and normal person. He did, however, seem to thrive on drama, pain, and fear. He seemed to run everything through his mind that was loaded with self-pity and pathological jealousy. He was a very toxic person in my life, and yes, no matter how smart I was, I was traumatized by him. This is what they call Narcissistic Abuse Syndrome. I learned what complicated post-traumatic stress disorder (CPTSD) was firsthand when dealing directly with a narc. It certainly was complicated!

> "To stop trying to communicate with a narc who
> is determined to misunderstand me is to win."
> —*a journal entry*

1c. Focus on Healing

> "To heal from his abuse is to win."
> —*a journal entry*

In all of my confusion and angst, I figured out the only right thing to do— which was sometimes the only thing that I could do— was to focus on my own healing. This life-saving skill was a muscle I had to develop. When I switched into "healing mode," I felt more stable and grounded in my own body. The inward focus was where I could get the truth and be healed by it, because nothing involving the narc ever helped me to heal.

> "To come back to myself is a win."
> —*a journal entry*

When I decided to write about the very difficult topic of co-parenting with a narcissist, I realized I was going to have to write about some very hard stuff. Examples include abuse of all kinds, child endangerment, child neglect, suicide, restraining orders, legal enforcement, and heart-breaking Family Court verdicts. I knew that the book may be filled with not only a sad reality, but also some horrible tragedy. However, I became willing to go into such a hard topic in order to help others who may be going through the same thing. At the time I am writing this, I personally know three separate friends dealing with this dilemma, themselves—all battling with a narc and losing sleep, money, and themselves, and they, too, have young children involved. Perhaps you are also like us—a mother who is getting your child returned to you injured, sick, and/or emotionally starved or stressed. If so, I am writing this for you.

"To share my wisdom is a win."
—a journal entry

It's a fact that co-parenting with a narc is not easy. Some experts claim it is inherently impossible, so they advise parallel parenting instead. Often, it feels like hell on earth to attempt either. Sometimes, when I'd allow myself to think about what I could have done with my life, I would feel really bad about the current state of my life, fall into self-pity, and regret having a child under these circumstances. I would have weeks of spontaneous crying and confiding in friends, whining to them that I felt like I had officially ruined my life by being associated with him in the past. He was a bad breakup that seemed to never end, because he wasn't just a co-parent who refused to put our child first and move on with his life, he was a full-on adversary, using our child for attention and the family courts for revenge, retaliation, and any abuse he could send my way. The worst of it was the guilt I felt for bringing a child into this world, under these conditions.

"The only thing worse than a narcissistic father, is a narcissistic mother. Thank God she has me."
—a journal entry

I craved a normal life because of all the hell and horror he posed. I thought that breaking up before ever finding out I was pregnant would somehow help me escape his disordered, untrustworthy self, but I soon learned that with Family Court and parental rights, there is generally no escaping when you have a child together. The options I had in front of me were to either leave my child behind and run away to a different state, or stay in town for my daughter and just try to stay away from him. While running to another state would save my life, I felt I could never do that. But, staying meant facing all the scrutiny, sabotage, adversity, abuse by proxy, lies, condemnation, accusations, chronic finger-pointing, and the like. Out of love, care, and concern for my daughter, I chose to stay, and therefore, it became a life-sentence. In choosing this option, my only recourse for survival was to do my healing work.

"As long as you are not in a codependent relationship with the narc, you are winning."
—a journal entry

1d. Make a Mantra

"To stay sane is a win."
—a journal entry

I had to learn to hang on, and hang in there. I loved my child, so much, and was so deeply committed to ensuring her health and safety, that I chose to stay. Sometimes, to face all the trials, I kept repeating phrases to myself as to why I would stay and get the crap kicked out of me, for lack of a better phrase. In desperation to stay clear-headed, I would create a mantra like, "I am doing this for her. I am doing this for her. I am doing this for her." That mantra helped me take the stand in a huge court trial where I was being accused of the worst types of things. Other times, I would say, "I am an adult. I can handle it. She is a child and needs the buffer." To keep my strength, new mantras—or mini-truths—would be developed when I had to take financial beatings through the court thrashings, AKA, abuse by proxy, I would say, "It's only money. This is her one-and-only childhood, so it's worth it."

"To stand up for my rights is a win."
—a journal entry

My dear friend Pat, who was married to a narc for twenty years and had three kids before getting a divorce was an option, would sometimes break out a paraphrased Bible quote and remind me that, "When you have done all that you can do, you are called to just stand." I did my best to stay standing on most days. Some days, it's all I could do.

During my research trying to figure out why the narc couldn't simply "play nice," I found that several experts noted how a narc needs a target, and boy . . . I sure knew I was it! For eight long years since breaking up with him on my terms, I had been his source of anger and reason for self-pity—in his black-and-white mind, that is. To be able to end that relationship, I had to gain enough self-love and recover from my own toxic codependency. It took me fifteen years of therapy—the entire length of our relationship—and thousands of group meetings to finally end the relationship with him for my own good. Not easy! And certainly not something I did overnight.

"To stay out of the relationship with the narc is to win."
—a journal entry

The only way I could get him to leave was when I said, "I just don't love you, anymore." That was how I got free. At the time, it was only half-true, because I hated his personality, but still loved him. I hated his lies, but still cared about him. It was the only lie I told him, but I feel like it saved my life. The deciding factor was that I grew to love me more than I loved him, and that became my overall win. Self-love was my solution.

> "To love myself even when I make a mistake is a win."
> —*a journal entry*

Before my recovery, I had the wrong mantras in place. I would say, "If only he quit drinking, things would be better. He would be better." I said that phrase way too many times over the years. I originally thought his drinking was my deal-breaker, and his drinking and driving were certainly appalling and unacceptable to me. I couldn't respect him for it. The day I realized that I was dealing with more than an alcoholic ex was the day my dear friend Pat said to me, very matter-of-factly, "He's trying to control you." I was shocked by her comment thrown at me so casually. I couldn't believe it at the time. At that point, I thought he was just a passive guy, as that was my general understanding of him after fifteen years. I truly had no idea he was controlling. He certainly wasn't the outwardly controlling type. Actually, I thought I was the controlling, worried, micromanaging mother who was being overly responsible. I had no idea what emotional abuse or manipulation was. I was shocked to discover just how he covertly controlled me using my fears and guilt. I put myself into counseling at a local domestic violence center and made my new mantra, "I am worth it!"

> "He might be continually poisoning his body with alcohol, but he is done poisoning my mind. That's a win!"
> —*a journal entry*

1e. Admit the Truth to Yourself

> "If I can tell myself the truth . . . that's a win."
> —*a journal entry*

My Two Major Personal Acknowledgments:

Pat often said that the truth will set me free. The day that I acknowledged that I was, 1) afraid of the narc, and 2) he was, indeed, controlling me in a roundabout, slick, and sly way, was the day he lost his power over me. And unfortunately, he knew it, and he picked up on it immediately at the very next exchange of our child. Once his spell over me was broken via Pat's words, I didn't speak to him for two whole years. Immediately after this, I caught him in a lie. The lie was so well orchestrated, so cleverly deceitful, that it was very similar to a 007 maneuver. At that time, he had a girlfriend that he didn't want me to know about, so to hide it from me, he would switch vehicles to pick-up our daughter to rendezvous with the new girl and her four children in a parking lot. What made the whole thing an even bigger circus was how I found out. I learned that a narc never wants to let people know about each other in case, 1) he could hoover me back for supply, or 2) we could find out about each other and share facts that would ultimately damage his character, and blow up his game.

> **"If I move on, even if he doesn't, that's a win."**
> *—a journal entry*

In an attempt to move on and have a healthy relationship, I started dating a nice man who had a daughter the same age as my daughter. Unfortunately, or fortunately for me, he complained about his ex, a lot. It was clear that he hadn't healed. I began to recognize similarities between his descriptions of his ex as a bad parent, and my ex's neighbor. After sorting through a few personal details with a bunch of, "Oh, my Gods," we converged on the same awful truth: our exes were together!

Armed with that knowledge, I learned all the tricky things my ex was up to that he hid from me so well. I finally had inside information on the mysterious, master manipulator, and just what he was up to behind the scenes. I won't get into the details of just how much I was being lied to, but let's just say it was interesting. I was now able to see him for who he really was: a brilliant actor, lying by omission without a conscience. The double whammy came when I recognized myself as being a hopeful, prone to denial, naive people-pleaser who was inclined to only see the best in people, and all my hindrances became his advantage!

> **"To wake up is a win. Even if it's painful and humiliating. I have another day to make a difference."**
> *—a journal entry*

After ending that short-term dating relationship and watching the narc's relationship inevitably fall apart, as well, I took a few years to grow in awareness of my flaws and change my thinking. I was afraid of confrontations; meanwhile, the narc loved them. I was an avid listener; he was a serial talker. I had to fundamentally change my thinking and my responses if I wanted to break the patterns of being lied to and used. I seemed to attract men who couldn't tell the truth, or were emotionally unavailable. I reflected on, and recognized my extreme levels of denial, my ability to romanticize everything, and my default mode of giving men the benefit of the doubt. I seriously considered my fears of confrontation and my inability to speak up for myself and make strong arguments. I had to change, heal, and advance my people-relating and communication skills. I had to take assertiveness classes because my people-pleasing nature made me a passive, easy victim of narcs.

> *"To change my past patterns is a win."*
> —*a journal entry*

1f. Mother

I witnessed the more serious effects of hopelessness and devastation caused by a narc in Family Court in my small town the year before COVID-19 broke out. A woman I knew—a sweet, loving mother of three boys—went through a divorce. Around Christmastime, the father was awarded custody of the sons while she got the house, and if you know anything about mothers, you'd understand we'd rather have our kids than anything else. She must have felt like her heart was ripped out of her, on top of being utterly humiliated because she worked with special needs children, and yet was not entitled to her own three sons. It was a crime what happened to her.

When the news circulated about her suicide death on Christmas Eve, our little isolated community felt rocked. Her pain must have been more than she could bear. I could feel her pain, because I was in almost the exact same place she was. I was going through a brutal custody battle during the holidays, myself, with the potential of losing my child to a narc.

> *"To know that I am not alone is a win."*
> —*a journal entry*

I also felt shock, horror, guilt, and grief, and I began to see that taking away a child from their mother is the ultimate injury that a narc attempts on his victims, when he has lost control of the relationship. It seems like narcs instinctively know a mother's values, and what we hold dear. It was a documented tactic even in the 1800s, and here it is, still being done in 2020. I decided to do my best as a mother, and forget how terrible he was as a father.

> *"To have women's rights is a win that he can't take away."*
> —*a journal entry*

That day, I vowed that no matter how bad the judge's final order may be, I was going to stay alive, because I realized that I was no good to my child dead. In my opinion, those three boys lost one of the most beautiful, precious souls—their hero. They were all in elementary school, all under the age of nine, and now forever subjected to their dad, with no mother to act as a buffer. I broke down in sobs remembering the last time I had encouraged her on the playground when she clearly looked depressed. I wish I had reached out to her. I wish I had told her where I was seeking help. I wish I had done more to support her, because I absolutely know that I cannot survive a narc attack, alone. I needed so much support to just keep me afloat, and I was thankful for everyone who helped me by throwing me a daily life raft. Too many times, well-meaning friends' advice was shallow, uneducated, and unhelpful, so I received the life raft emotional support I needed from wise elders and experts.

The truth was . . . I wasn't dealing with a normal, rational, caring person; I was dealing with a shark. In another attempt to understand the interactions between us, I developed a powerful shark analogy. Sharks are predators, and in my view, so are narcs. They are social predators, and in my younger years, I was a type of "social prey." I was vulnerable narc food with very few self-protection resources, because sharks hunt vulnerable targets for food. They live meal-to-meal, so they need their next meal just to stay alive. They aren't warm, friendly, and fuzzy. The similarities astounded me.

Only a young, stealthy seal can escape the jaws of a shark, and even its zigzag swim doesn't always work. I have seen smart seals swim behind the shark to stay out of view for a while and gather their strength, before making a mad dash for escape, which, of course, made me cheer. In my situation, I either had to get out of the water, or learn to swim sideways like a seal, and I had to do my best to mother our child under these run-or-get-eaten circumstances. I had done my zigzag swim in Family Court for eight tiring years. It was time to tread water behind him and gain my strength back.

> **"I am forty years old and it feels like I am fighting for my life. The narc is a shark."**
> —*a journal entry*

I knew that I had to get healthy. Healthy mothers are so important. I made it my mission to be the best mother that I could be for her. This meant staying alive, staying healthy, asking for help, and focusing on my wins.

> **"For my child to have a mother is a win."**
> —*a journal entry*

To give myself hope and maybe find a chink in the armor of a narc, I did more research on sharks. Yes, real sharks. To my delight and surprise, I learned that a pod of orca whales can team up, kill, and eat a shark. However,

I learned that they had to be persistent and work together by communicating underwater with each other to be able to do this incredible feat. I was gaining valuable information by thinking in symbolic terms and watching how nature worked. I learned that a shark had to always be moving to keep oxygen flow in its gills, or it would die, and orcas knew this secret. They would surround and corral a shark by hunting it in a pack. Then, one brave orca would hit it in the side, flip it upside down, and hold it completely still for a few minutes until it lost air. Watching this on animal videos gave me a strange sense of hope. I needed to call in the orcas, because I felt like I was dealing with a shark.

> "To ask for expert help is a win."
> —*a journal entry*

Just as important as calling in the orcas, I needed to have a life while I was swimming in the shark's shadow, waiting until I had the strength I needed to be her mother. I didn't want a life of shark hunting or narc-sitting (adult babysitting) for us. I found that the most incredible freedom is the freedom from a toxic person. I wanted to savor that, and cherish that victory, so I began to take breaks from the battle and come back to my own life. I learned to have fun with my child, even though I felt sad. I learned to cherish her childhood, even though it was tainted with my blood. I did my best to keep our life as wonderful and full as it could be when she was with me.

> "To make our life our focus is to win."
> —*a journal entry*

Establish Self-Rule #1 - Switch Focus and Survive (If you have been victimized, used, or abused, it's important to recognize that. It's equally important to recognize that you are now a survivor. To move past victim, and into surviving we have to make a mental shift. Then, we can more into thriving and become wiser and stronger than before.)

Self-Reflection Questions:

- How can you best survive your situation?
- Is there a "survivor mindset" that you can adopt?

Self-Rule #2

LEARN TO COEXIST

"Life-saving tip #1 to self: learn to live with the problems."
—a journal entry

At the start of the 2020 COVID-19 global pandemic, I realized that I was just one of 7.6 billion people on the earth. When the realization struck me that I was only one of many, I recognized how minuscule my existence was. On that day, one hundred thousand Americans had died from the coronavirus already, yet I was still alive at age forty after having a strange cough for two months, and a host of other unidentifiable symptoms. I felt very powerless against the virus. Against the world, I felt small and insignificant. It was eerily similar to how I felt facing a fueled-up, ready-to-attack, angry narcissist. The narc. My ex. My child's father.

"There is a virus among us and I think it's the narc."
—a journal entry

I felt lucky to have survived the pandemic. I felt blessed and grateful. I also felt a strange type of confusion. What was going on in the world? This wasn't how I imagined life would be in America. I also wondered just what was happening in my world? This wasn't how I imagined raising a child would turn out. I was living in a world that I didn't like.

A few months before the pandemic struck, I lost legal custody of my only child to a narc. After losing custody of my young daughter in Family Court, I needed to digest that experience and make some sense out of it, so I looked at my situation from every possible angle. The narc had used some cleverly deceitful tactics, combined with an expensive legal game, to win under false pretenses. I needed to smarten up . . . somehow.

After the brutal loss, I went into deep introspection. I spent months in serious contemplation that was very similar to a "dark night of the soul." It is a very intense spiritual crisis of meaning and existence that a person can fall into in any given situation. In that darkness, I couldn't see my way forward. I desperately wanted to protect my child, so I reflected on my entire messed-up story, took a time-out from life, and paused to see what I could observe. I was trying to get a firm mental grip on something so slippery—the narc's game—and that's when I came up with a creative way to view my problem.

A New View of My Problem

I tried to see in terms of symbols, instead of the obvious tragic reality. Sometimes in an attempt to understand the details of things, I think in larger terms. Since so many online programs were available, I knew that I wasn't the only one dealing with a narcissist. Every year, new books were published by psychological experts on narcs. There were also blogs, videos, and plenty of court crisis materials on dealing with narcs, since they posed such a threat to children, always demanded all the assets in a divorce, and loved conflict. There was a high demand for help with narcs, so I knew that I wasn't alone with this particular problematic type of person. I also believed that what happens in the micro, happens in the macro, and vice versa. I began to wonder how narcissism played out in the larger world, and not just in my personal life.

White Blood Cells and The Body of Humanity

To get clarity, I tried to step out of the struggle with the narcissist and see from a higher vantage point. I wanted to understand what was happening to me. I was losing my power and energy, and I wanted to recover from my losses and tragedy. I started to think visually and symbolically. Since I realized how small I was in the world, I considered myself much like a cell in the body of humanity, and as I got to know myself better, I saw how much of an innate fixer, care-taker, and helper I was.

If I were to accurately identify myself, I would consider myself some type of white blood cell. White blood cells are part of the body's immune system, always working to clean up problems. I began to imagine humanity as a whole body, with all types of unique people working in different specific areas. The visual that I started generating was very similar to the inside of the body where the heart does its job, the brain does its job, and the blood pumps through other cells doing all their individual jobs, simultaneously. Even smaller than those major organs, which are comprised of many cells with the same mission, were the individual blood cells circulating in the bloodstream doing certain special jobs. In my view, everybody in the world is like a cell, doing its function in the body to, 1) protect the body, and 2) keep it running. In terms of society, people doing their jobs well, protect our civilization. I was a part of this, no matter how small.

A Virus?

In the Al-Anon program, which I attended for twenty years, they talked about alcoholism being a disease. Well, I thought . . . if alcoholism is a disease, then narcissism must be a virus. I started to wonder about the true nature of narcissism, because it really seemed like a virus to me. It took and took, it acted on its own, without caring about anything else, and it moved on quickly to a new target/source/host when it burned a bridge. The narc seemed out of place and out of step with helping humanity. From all my research on narcissism, it seemed like there was no cure, for they typically never admitted that they needed help. All he cared about was himself, and in his eyes, he was without fault.

The Virus Among Us

So, to me, narcissism seemed like a foreign invader taking up a ton of social resources in society. He didn't fit nicely and cooperatively into the organized body of society. To deal with the narc, I had to use the law and the courts because, as far as I could see, he just didn't want what was best for others. I also had to use the support of friends and the people around me to help keep the narc- virus in check and myself stable. Nothing ever cured him. Every day, he just kept being himself, somehow blending in and causing problems for me and others. He wasn't going away, and no one could stop him. Or so it seemed.

For several years, in an attempt to coerce cooperation, I attended a Non-Violent Communication group, asking how I could get through to him so we could co-parent together. After following all those suggestions and still receiving zero teamwork on his part, it was then clear he only wanted to work against me, and for himself. After learning this, I started asking a better question: "How do I stop enabling?" I then asked the group, "What is the opposite of enabling?" I asked because I realized that all my love and help . . . just enabled the narc to continue existing in a lie. To my surprise, a wise old man of the group, a therapist for thirty-plus years, spoke up very calmly and softly, saying, "You kill it . . . the exact opposite of enabling, is to kill."

I was really shaken at his remark because, for me, that wasn't a good answer. It certainly wasn't something that I was willing to do. I just wanted to improve my situation with an adversarial co-parent. But, then, I remembered all the thousands of Al-Anon meetings that I attended. I remembered all the angry, frustrated, rage-filled, and hopeless women with children who would sometimes blurt out, "I just want to kill him!" I never really believed they would, even with all the tears streaming down their red faces. Instead, I passed their comment off as just a venting episode that happens when one feels like the whole damn thing is impossible. I considered it a momentary feeling that just needed to be expressed, not actually something they were plotting. I knew they loved their alcoholics and were trying everything to survive all the problems alcoholism brought with it. Now, knowing a little more about viruses and how the body fights disease, I think they may have been onto something. It isn't so farfetched to talk about killing the problem, since it was continually generating more problems; nature and biology are designed to do this.

So, getting back to the body . . . I realized that in order for the body to be in harmony, everything has to be doing its job, and first and foremost, systems have to be safe to allow them to do so. In order to remain safe, the body needs certain protection cells to defend against viruses or invaders, and there are many types of white blood cells to do this job. These cells are called natural killer cells. There are many more types of immune system cells, and I found them all fascinating. They all have special jobs to fight against viruses.

All these types of white blood cells comprise the body's different immune response systems. I noted that, just like the body, we have police, jails, hospitals for the sick, laws, and nurses and doctors to help treat sick people, all fighting to keep society healthy. When I looked at myself, I realized if I were a white blood cell, I would be classified as a lymphocyte.

Typically, lymphocytes surround the virus and pull it out of the body. They are like a search-and-destroy cell, or search-and-fix cell when they encounter a virus. For me, the work it took to fix situations was burning me out, and I wasn't willing to make that effort anymore. I had pulled back my energy of loving the narc into health and wholeness, since it wasn't working. This new phase of surviving narcissism was all about saving myself and neutralizing the threat by calling in others for support. I was like the white blood cell that kept running back to the home base—the lymph node—and asking what type of antibodies they had that would neutralize this threat. I would take some solutions and apply them to the problems, only to see the narc generate more problems.

Unfortunately, he would mutate. The narc was an expert shapeshifter. At this point, I realized that I was not dealing with a simple problem, because those problems can have solutions. Instead, I was dealing with a complicated predicament. This type of predicament didn't have a simple solution, so basically, I felt stuck.

When I studied immunity to learn more about it, it became more interesting to learn that there were memory lymphocytes called b-lymphocytes that remembered certain viruses and were kept around just in case. By writing my book, I felt like I was performing a b- lymphocyte's job.

I was keeping the memory alive of what a narc is capable of, and alerting other cells/mothers. Other similarities that were amazing to learn were how a part of the virus would be taken back to the lymph node for analysis, and then antibodies would be constructed from that informational material. I felt that every time I attended a Twelve-Step meeting and shared how horrible the newest drama was, I was returning to the lymph node with part of my problem, asking for anyone who had experienced this before, and how to fix or cure it. When I learned that white blood cells would attach themselves to the virus to disable it, I realized that I was just doing what a white blood cell does—attaching! It was even more interesting to note that white blood cells sometimes have to detach or die with the virus. I certainly had to detach from the narc, or die. I was amazed at the body's intricate system for dealing with viruses, and how many mechanisms were in place for different invaders. I had to learn from how the body operated to see if there was a more natural course for me to take to be able to survive a narc. I contemplated the body's wisdom.

> **"At this point, I have to detach from the narc or die."**
> —*a journal entry*

So, here I was, stuck with a narc as a co-parent, pretty sure he was a virus, and I couldn't find a peaceful cure. The family courts couldn't even detect him. However, I could, and over the years, I learned to develop antibodies and immunity for myself against his tactics and tricks. I recognized that the longer people got to know him—and our horrible, lengthy, high conflict story—the more they saw the truth of the matter. That was usually when he would move onto new people and environments where he couldn't be detected. See how well a virus knows how to survive? I guessed that he instinctively knew how to survive by keeping everyone fooled, but the lies couldn't add up to truth forever. Over time, if a bunch of us caught onto the uncooperative destructive nature, we would surround him. It is very similar to the type of immune response that the body uses to fight off serious infection. Everyone has to work together to be effective. Imagine if we all developed the discipline to detect and discern problems before they infiltrated finances, marriages, and children's minds. This is how I discovered the enormous benefits of seeing symbolically.

> **"I am now immune from entering into a toxic relationship with a narc. My radar is ready, and my identifying skills are sharp. There are so many out there!"**
> —*a journal entry*

Learning to "Live and Let Live"

There is a slogan in Al-Anon: "Live and Let Live." I decided I wasn't willing to destroy myself to fix him, and I wasn't willing to spend all my time circling him and working on him. Knowing I was expected by the family courts to hand a child over to him—a person I deemed unsafe—caused me so much sadness, grief, guilt, and fear. After suffering through these emotions and deciding I couldn't do the opposite of enabling, I realized there was no effective solution. I would have to learn to coexist with the narc. That became my answer.

I realize that everyone's situation may be different, with different levels of malignant narcs, but I didn't want our daughter to be without a mother and a father. The court's policy was that a child benefited from the resources of both a mother and a father, and I, in agreement, didn't want her to be disadvantaged. I was humble enough to know that I was a human with flaws, too. I knew that the coronavirus didn't just take out the wicked, evil people of the earth, and that I was vulnerable to the global health threat, too. What if something happened to me? Did I want her to be an orphan? No.

I also realized that although the narc hated me, he loved his daughter in the way that he could. Or, at least he "owned" her in his mind, and it followed that as she was "his," she would be somewhat cared for. He saw her as a source of supply, meaning, and purpose. It wasn't the type of love that I gave her, the type of love that I would judge as "good," but he still showed up for his parenting time. I often questioned his reasons for taking on this duty, because quite often, to my shock and horror, he was borderline neglectful of his duties as a parent. Sometimes she was harmed by this. Sometimes she suffered. However, after eight years in court, I wasn't able to prove it. The harm was never blatant enough, and emotional abuse is very difficult to prove. What's worse is that his wealthy parents applauded him for having a child. He gained a ton of approval, even if all he did was the minimum. Parental enabling can last a lifetime. Up against his parents' enabling and everything their money could buy, I became victimized every time I got into the ring with him. A friend told me, "Don't wrestle with pigs, because you both get muddy, and the pig enjoys it!"

What Could I Do Now?

I had to come to terms with why I lost in court. I had to face all my regrets. The bottom line was that I was a victim of the many narc tactics, and what his parents' money could buy. Due to the global pandemic, the family courts were shut down, so my situation wasn't going to change for the time being. This gave me an added opportunity to try to see my situation in a new light. I really couldn't affect what happened in the past. So, what could I do now? I tried talking to myself on many long walks, crying on the phone to my therapists, and complaining to compassionate friends.

After the dust of the latest court order settled, I realized that what I could do was go forward with a healthy new approach and make new choices. I knew that my mindset meant everything, for I had observed how my mindset determined my emotional state. Every single thought in my head generated a coinciding feeling. I had felt hopeless for the past three months, and I wanted to change. So I decided to change. The first word that came to me in my daily meditation was "survive." In order to survive a virus, I needed a balanced emotional state, as well as a good immune system.

Modulating My Response

As we learned with COVID-19, many deaths were due to an overactive immune system response. I certainly was guilty of overreacting to every single thing the narc did wrong. I learned that I needed to moderate my approach, or risk using up all my energy and resources at once. That was certain death in Family Court. My attorney advised me that I had to start thinking about the long game. In my viral research, I learned that sometimes a body can't clear certain viruses completely, so it learns to coexist with viruses such as HIV and tuberculosis. That's what I needed to do in the midst of a global pandemic with the family courts being closed. That's what I needed to do with a narc, too.

As I studied, basically by watching expert YouTube videos, and reading extensive medical articles, I learned more about viruses than I ever expected. I learned how some viruses get into the cytoplasm and make copies of itself to infect the host, which the body can eventually clear with a good immune system. Then I discovered how other, trickier viruses get into the DNA and can never be cleared by the body. In those cases, the body must learn to function around the infection. I was beginning to draw some parallels that sent my mind reeling.

"Detach or die!"
—a journal entry

To regain my mental health and strength, I needed to charge my batteries, restore, refresh, replenish, and realign to my own nature. I survived a costly, stressful three-and-a-half year legal war and a five-day trial. Meanwhile, being attached to the narc via that court trial felt like a slow death. He accused me of everything, and it felt like I was being shot at with accusation after accusation. The court situation often felt utterly hopeless. He was the pig who liked to throw mud. That saying always reminded me how unpleasant it was to be involved with a narc. Every conversation was a mud-slinging match. Actually, every interaction with a narc was that way, and I hated getting dirty.

The truth is that the narc liked causing trouble. It energized him, yet drained me. What do you do with a troublemaker who enjoys making trouble? That was a riddle that I asked all the experts.

This is when they all advised me to do my "work." This required not just the practice of detachment, but also the skill of quickly letting go as soon as I realized I was hanging on again. I learned how to let go. I learned how to "Live and Let Live." I would often find myself caught up in conflict and trouble with the narc while co- parenting. Instead, I needed to follow some principles. I needed my own set of ground rules when interacting with him, since dealing with him as I would a normal person wasn't effective. Rules with him never worked. He couldn't follow my rules. He actually made up his own rules and did whatever he wanted, anyway. I saw real growth when I began to back out of dealings with him.

What could acceptance do for me?

Wise people kept advising me to do my work and stop trying to work on him. Well-meaning mentors told me to simply accept the situation as bad. This was very difficult for my pride to do. I had learned the hard way that conversations with him couldn't help. The narc never cared about my feelings, that being the fundamental nature of his disorder, so I had to accept his many limitations. I accepted that he couldn't care about humanity, me, or our child. I also learned to accept the awful situation. Accepting the sucky situation, that of having to co-parent with a narc, was the ultimate paradigm shift for me. Accepting that I couldn't change him was one thing, but accepting that I had a sucky situation that I could do very little about was another. Acceptance allowed me to move forward in a healthy way. Once the paradigm shift took place inside of me, when it entered my body and not just my fearful over-worked mind, I felt freer to live my life. After all, I wanted the "live" part of "Live, and Let Live." I longed to do my own quality living. That was the shift. That was how I came to the conclusion that I needed to coexist with a narc.

I found this virus and body analogy very helpful moving forward. As I identified what was happening in the conflict with a narc, I became smarter about the issues. I learned what flying monkeys are, what minions are, what gaslighting is, and how poisoning the well, really does sway good people's minds. I was able to identify all the strategies the narc used to get away with things. More importantly, I was able to identify the "helper response" in me to every crisis he created.

With my narcissist recovery, I began putting the focus on me. I began having the power to choose from a healthy place as I gradually recovered from the abuse and victimization. My power came back to me when I owned who I was. From there, I was able to decide how I was going to live my life. I started to make new choices of what to do with a valuable lymphocyte life.

The rest of this book contains my survival strategies that I use to cope and live with the problem of narcissism. May you find techniques that work for the predicament in your life. Perhaps this knowledge will help you level the playing field in the legal game or the game of life. As they say at all those helpful meetings—AKA lymph nodes—"Take what you like, and leave the rest."

Establish Self-Rule #2 - Learn to Co-Exist (Adopt a mindset that is not black and white, all or nothing, you versus them. Make your mind up that since the courts grant rights, you will have to accept this fact even if it goes against your moral code and principles. Have your mind made up to make the best of any bad situations. Essentially, you learn to live with the problem person vs. find ways to eliminate them if this risks your custody case and you don't have enough evidence and backing from CPS to do anything about it.)

Self-Reflection Questions:

- Can you see the need to coexist as co-parents?
- How do you define your own freedom?
- How can you detach from a toxic situation or thought?

Self-Rule #3

LEARN TO LIVE WITH THE WINS

"I lost so badly in court! Or did I?"
—a journal entry

Facing a battle with a narc meant that my mindset was everything to me, and it still is. I knew that it would not only determine my experience of going through something like this, but also the actual outcome. I have heard that saying, "What you see is what you get," and I felt like it completely applied in my circumstance. If I chose to only see all my losses, then I would get buried in the overwhelming loss. On the other hand, if I kept my focus on the wins, I would be energized and inspired. The small victories in Family Court kept my hope alive—that me and my child would both be okay.

"I won a few important things this round, but is it enough to keep my child safe?"
—a journal entry

At this point, I had done enough personal growth work to know that there were two ways of thinking. I identified them both in simple terms. There was fear-based thinking, and love-based thinking. I had to choose which one I wanted to adopt every day. During this time, I had a wonderful therapist who was very knowledgeable about the human brain. Every counseling session, I learned something new about my brain organ. She would tell me about neurological receptors and how they function. She was fascinated by how we used our brain organ, and would always remind me to use my brain well.

"Being brave enough to use court . . . is a win."
—a journal entry

She was always very concerned about what I was telling myself. She always wanted to know what my thoughts were up to. She would point out her concern if my thoughts were straying into negative thinking, because she believed it drove me into despair and depression. She would always point out that I had a choice in picking my thoughts, and that the cycle of bad thinking could be interrupted by different tools and tricks. Basically, she handed me back the power to choose my thoughts about everything in my life, and I desperately wanted my power back.

> **"I know that having me fall apart on her would be worse than what I just lost in court. I need to keep myself together. That will mean everything to her. How I handle this will matter more. Can I live with this pain? Can I do it gracefully?"**
>
> *—a journal entry*

My support groups were valuable places for me to unload some of my pain and share my story with other people. Most of the members of these groups could identify with my problems.

Unfortunately, they, too, had met a narc once or twice in their lifetime. One particular group was comprised of several therapists and people who specialized in court, children, and family. I valued their input and wisdom greatly. However, each week of my three-and-a-half year crisis, they grew more and more helpless regarding my unfair court dilemma. At one point, the moderator of the group said that he felt so helpless that there was nothing he could do. He asked very abruptly what I needed from the group. How does the group help me? I could only say that I needed someone to hear my story and watch me endure it. I knew there was nothing they could do, no matter their profession. I could tell that the moderator felt sad to hear my tragedy as I went through pain after pain, injury after injury, week after week. It wasn't until months after the trial that he heard me say that I had learned something valuable. He felt overjoyed to hear that I had personal growth of any kind. That's when I realized that my growth is what mattered most.

About a year earlier, he had asked me how I felt. As I searched inside myself, I realized that I didn't know. I confessed that I had been too busy putting out fires that the narc started, and too busy helping my child with special needs and raising her on my own, that I hadn't had a moment to even feel. I was in crisis mode and hardly had any time to myself to feel any emotions. I would get a short break to take care of running my life and do the laundry, then get my child back with bruises and injuries, so I only had time to act. Being in crisis mode for all those years left very little time to sit around and just feel my feelings. I was raising a child with a narc, and he was working against me. He counter-parented me, which drained all my energy, and caused people to ignore our child's needs. That was the worst tragedy of all—that her needs went overlooked because of all the narc's tactics, antics, and drama. With only half-custody now, I finally had time to feel, and the emotional tidal wave drowned me for six months. I had a backlog of feelings that I never had time to feel. I would cry in the grocery store, in the shower, and standing in the kitchen cooking. Everywhere.

> **"This experience is so painful that even other people hurt when they hear my story. I feel guilty for triggering them. I now acknowledge that those who haven't healed fully can't hear my story."**
> *—a journal entry*

Another loving elderly member, who had struggles of her own and usually didn't speak up much, asked me a very powerful question one day in a soft voice. Practically whispering, she asked if I could, "Learn to live with the wins, for now?" After the unfavorable judgment, in my clouded defeated mind, I thought, "Hey! That's a thought!" I knew that I needed to invest in a better attorney going forward, and that the judge had already issued his ruling. So basically, there was nothing that I could do for the time being. Then, on my meditation walk, I also heard a higher power tell me to "list your wins." The list that I made that day boosted my morale and resolve to keep going. That list was a game-changer. I pinned it to the forefront of my mind, and on the front inside page of all my journals. I had won on so many accounts, and not just what the judge granted me. They were small victories in this great big war.

The wins far exceeded the loss, simply because some of the wins were personal and permanent. For example, I would never again trust a narcissist, or get into an abusive relationship with one. I would take legal action and use the courts, which I was afraid to do initially. I would call child protection agencies if something was happening that was abusive or neglectful. I would undergo scrutiny and bullying in Family Court and not give in to agreements, just to try to appease a never-satisfied narc. I would live on my own and be financially independent by asking for help, even if that meant humbling myself to go to the local food bank. I wouldn't be tortured by a narc's statements about me; instead, I would confront them and ask for cooperation—something he was inherently incapable of. It was also a big foundational win that I knew what type of animal I was dealing with, and that I could educate myself on the topic, whereas before, I couldn't figure out why he was being so mean, cold, cruel, selfish, self-centered, and crazy. He was a narc, through and through. I was going to get what a narc had to give whenever I dealt with his disordered self.

"The harsh reality: I can't protect my child from everything."
—a journal entry realization

No matter what, I had to learn to live with the outcome of the courts—for now. It wasn't easy for a while. It felt like I couldn't breathe, eat, or sleep. What happened at my trial really disturbed me deep down into my soul. I would go over and over all the mistakes my attorney made, all the clever tactics his attorney used, the narc's performance on the stand, my performance, the interruptions, the continuances, etc. It was so mentally consuming, and bogged me down for months and months. My brain just wanted to figure it all out. My brain wanted to fix it. My brain wanted to do its job, and keep me and my child safe against a known threat. My brain was overworked and stressed. It needed a rest, and that is why I started meditating regularly.

"My healing journey will take time. It will take some time to see the wins in my situation clearly. The pain is too much to bear most days."
—a journal entry

I also did other things to keep my mind from ruminating and sliding down into an inevitable pain spiral. I tried to just live a normal life on days she was not with me. It felt like the wind was knocked out of me with a sucker punch to take my young daughter away for six days in a row, but I had to "lump it" and keep walking and breathing. It felt incredibly hard to live without her. She was my primary reason for existing for the past nine years. She was my purpose. I felt the void and felt crushed. It took a while to learn to enjoy the void. I went through the natural grieving stages and cycles. It took time to move from disbelief to acceptance. If you are not familiar with the typical stages of grief, I highly recommend you master them so that they can be moved through more quickly. I was only able to achieve effectiveness with the narc by processing grief like a pro.

Learning to live again in a new way with the new schedule was a difficult battle. It took months to get used to the time to myself. I didn't even know what to do with all the free time. I was used to catering to a young child's needs; now, I was worried if her needs were even being met by the narc. I tried not to think about her and felt guilty when I was successful for an hour. I tried to entertain my mind with all kinds of things to keep steady throughout the lonely days.

I also tried to stop focusing on the problems and start focusing on the solution. I knew that I had to move forward. I had to take a new approach in court because defending myself continually against his accusations was not only exhausting, but also made me look guilty. I bought online legal programs to learn how to do it myself. It felt so beyond my abilities to represent myself in a pro se manner. I had already witnessed how complicated the legal system was, so I knew that I would need an attorney.

To start a new chapter in Family Court, I consulted new expensive attorneys, not knowing how I could ever afford them. I was particularly in despair when one attorney said that she wouldn't take me as a client, because it was too high conflict. That's when it hit me that maybe no one would want my problems, that possibly, no legal professional would help me correct this. I went into despair for a whole month over that rejection. However, other national attorneys that specialized in narcissism told me to keep calling around. They were sure that someone would take my case and help me. So I did. I called and asked and paid hundreds and thousands of dollars for new legal advice. Finally, an attorney agreed to take me, and my case, on. However, it hit especially hard to hear that I couldn't reverse the judgment. That we could only go forward and wait for something big and bad to happen. That was horrifying to hear. The whole reason I was fighting to keep her in my custody was to prevent something bad from happening.

During my legal research, I had one attorney tell it to me straight. She had been in the family law business for over thirty years and supervised all the family law lawyers in her firm. She told me that if the other party is willing to lie, cheat, and steal to win, then they will eventually get their way, and there was nothing I could do about that. It was after that phone call that I realized just what the narc was capable of. At that point, he had successfully sabotaged me at all five of her pediatricians' offices, and dangerously portrayed me as a mother who had Munchausen syndrome by proxy. It was a serious allegation, and his complaints caused professionals to turn and suspect me of the most horrible things. That night, I had an "ah-ha" moment. I realized that it was good for him to have sole legal custody for now, because if he continued to lie to professionals in private meetings, I was getting dangerously close to having DCF show up at my door and take her abruptly, and possibly permanently, away. I knew that there were mothers in similar situations who were losing their children in this type of traumatic manner to the narcs. My brave battle in court was much better than that scenario. It would have been so traumatic for my child and me to endure that type of event happening. By him having sole legal custody, he could complain all he wanted to professionals, but I had no more say, and, therefore, couldn't be harming her with doctor's appointments. This was a very tricky way to live. Living in the shadow of a narc's lies was depressing, to say the least.

> "How do I live with the fact that I can't change what happened in court?"
> —*a journal entry*

Creating a New Life

I had to find a way to live. I needed to create a life for myself. It was a new chapter, possibly a new series. A new adventure that I never saw coming—where I was only a part-time parent, and the other half of my life, I was a single person with no responsibilities or rights to my child. After eight years of being a mom, I didn't know how to live selfishly and just think about me for half the month. It was so foreign that I was basically sitting around my apartment, waiting for her to come home to start living again. Nothing got done. Nothing was accomplished. I just waited to be able to live and go back to my life. That is when I realized that I needed to do something meaningful with all this spare time.

I had once complained to a recovery program friend that the one thing that I felt like I never did "right" in my life was to live selfishly. I would vent with anger that if I had to do it over again, I would just spend money on myself and think about myself. I would argue that I wasn't the one with problems, so why should I have to stick around and deal with people who have them? My ex, the narc, had the problems. My child had special needs, and I was always dealing with those. I lost sleep, time, money, and myself all in the name of helping those who needed help, as well as dealing with people who were so disordered and unable to cooperate. I felt like I didn't deserve any of it, and if I was just left to be by myself, I would be just fine. Now, here I was, by myself, and I had to learn how to live this way.

When the fire of anger burned down, I started to notice the gifts in the void. I noticed that it was peaceful, quiet, and simple without a child in my living space. I started to value solitude and time to myself. I started to imagine things that I could do with my time. Enjoyable things. This healing process took time.

Where's the problem?

Since I was so heavily bogged down in the narc court conflict, I often didn't know where the problem was coming from. I had to figure out to what degree my current problem was being generated from within, and to what degree it was outside of myself. Sometimes the problem was inside of me as much as outside of me. The problem of my fears and projections that caused anxiety was coming from within. The incidents of harm to the child were happening outside of myself. I had to be clear about where exactly the problems were so that I could effectively address them.

The Needs of the Present Moment

I learned to ask myself, "What are my needs at this moment?" I practiced staying true to the present moment whenever I would lose myself in planning a new legal strategy. I didn't want to abandon the legal process, but given that I couldn't change the legality of it in the moment, I tried to return to the present and feel safe. A woman at my local church who suffered tremendously forty years prior and lost her children to a narc, was very shaken by my story. She would often just cry when attempting to help me, because she knew all too well the pain and anguish. She, too, was powerless. She advised me to learn to accept that, "This is what it is." She encouraged me not to focus my life on lawsuits. She mentioned that my inner life has to realize the outer results, and learn to live with the conclusion. With tears streaming down her face, she asked me if I wanted to pursue more legal action and be in a legal process forever. She asked me, "How can you relax into the outcome and let it be?" I knew her pain was deep and ancient.

Others in the church agreed with her, that constantly dealing with legal matters would drain my soul. They wondered if there was a way for me to separate the legal process I needed to take from the rest of my life. Could I keep the two separate so that I could not only function, but enjoy my life with my child, too? How could I maintain living in the moment while still petitioning the court for rights to my child and justice? Some members felt that they weren't mutually exclusive. More seasoned members on conscious paths that included the study of Buddhism and activism said to consider doing both. It would certainly take great skill in trying. I would need a great awareness of myself. Of course, I realized the potential freedom of not being tied to legal problems. It was always a momentary fantasy to move away to a tropical island and leave it all behind, but I refused to leave my child behind.

> "I feel like I failed my child. I feel like I failed
> as a mother to protect her—even though I
> know that the systems failed us both."
> —*a journal entry*

Feelings

What I had to do was deal with my feelings like a therapist would. I learned to be my own loving, listening therapist when it came to tough emotions. Acceptance is what allowed me to not be controlled by my strong emotions. The logic was that if I owned the feeling, I had the ability to let it go. Conversely, if the feeling had me, then I couldn't let it go. I had to feel, but not be dominated, nor controlled by my feelings. I had to allow the feelings to rise and fall like a wave, but not get caught in the break of them, nor the undertow. Sitting in the comfy recliner chair, I had to be like the serene person on the beach, watching the waves reach the shore and dissolve. I had to gain masterful control of my mind and emotions to be able to handle the outcomes of the legal battles and raising a child with a narc. At times, it felt like I was on the shore watching a hurricane conjure up waves so tall that they would swallow me if I got too close.

My Needs

The small church group was very valuable to me, especially in helping me identify my needs. I needed a sense of safety and connection with my child. I had to be careful to make sure that I wasn't strategizing to get my needs met through the narc. The narc wasn't someone that could meet my needs. On the other hand, court and the legal interventions could—at least in some ways.

> **"I must learn to live with the wins from court, since there is no winning with the narc."**
> *—a journal entry*

Establish Self-Rule #3: Learn to Live with the Wins (Write down what you have won even if it's just your freedom from your ex. Being free of a toxic relationship, healed or in healing, allows you to be a healthy parent. Adopt a winning mindset to look closely and regularly at the positives in your custody situation. Know that motions for a change of custody order, in most cases, can be filed by either party going forward. NOTE: This varies upon circumstances. But a "Final Order" rarely is ever final due to the rights of both parties to file for an adjustment, change, or a specific request. Know your rights and what qualifies. If going immediately back to court on an appeal, or motion isn't in your best interest, then have patience. Learn to live in the "meantime" and make the best of it.)

Self-Reflection Questions:

- List your wins. What do you have going for you and your child/children?
- List your gratitudes. What are you thankful for when it comes to your life?
- What do you like about your life?

Self-Rule #4

KEEP THE FOCUS ON LOVE

"The only true freedom is love."
—*a journal entry*

There was no question that I loved my child. As a mother, I wanted to protect her innocence, youth, and childhood from the narc. Mostly, I wanted to keep her safe. I was willing to do whatever it took. I was the "mama bear." When she was really little, she had some special needs/developmental delays, so I worked overtime to get her the services and help the specialist recommended. I went above and beyond for her out of love. I even quit my job to be able to stay home with her, because she struggled at daycare. It was so much work to raise her, but it was a labor of love. My actions proved that I clearly loved her, but did I love myself?

"I can't see any of myself when I am always looking at them and what they need/require."
—*a journal entry*

I recall the moment that I learned her father was a narc. It was about three years into the family court drama when my easy-going attorney made a passing comment about him. As we were sitting in a hallway after yet another round in court, I expressed my frustration that I couldn't understand why my ex was so unreasonable, and wanted it all. My attorney, who had a background in psychology, then told me very casually that my ex was a narcissist. From that statement forward, I researched narcs to learn the meaning of the mess I was in and how to cope. From that point on, I knew what I was up against. This became an intellectual advantage.

> **"There is so much online information on narcissists in court custody battles! What's going on here!? I see a big problem and a real pattern!"**
> —*a journal entry*

With all the focus on my child and the narc, I never looked at myself. At one point in parenting, I started to question if I loved myself, because I was being blamed for everything and not being treated well by anyone, yet I was still standing there, getting battered and bruised—taking it all. My ex's unhappiness and my daughter's high maintenance needs all fell on my shoulders. I was sleep-deprived, dealing with our child's inability to sleep on my own, catering to all her special needs, just to get dressed or ride in a car, swerving his inability to cooperate, and dodging his thirst for vengeance, all while actively witnessing his use of the court system to reclaim his self-esteem. I took the brunt of both of their issues and inabilities. It felt like I was getting hit from both sides, and while I did my best to shield myself, I had no support system to help me. Unfortunately, my parents were uneducated, ill-equipped, mentally unarmed, and lacked the resources to help. Basically, they didn't want to step into the mess with me and get it on their shoes. I was at the point of hating the narc, and hating my life.

> **"Hating the narc is a jail. It's pure self-imprisonment. I am just going to mentally walk away."**
> —*a journal entry*

To water my dry and weary soul, a generous friend gifted me a weekend women's spiritual retreat, and the retreat leader opened with a powerful question that I will never forget, and still use to this day. She asked us to do a journaling exercise to begin our weekend and set the theme. She offered the prompt, "If I were a woman who loved myself, I would . . . ," and asked us to fill in the blank.

> **"Why do I stumble on self-love? It always trips me up."**
> —*a journal entry*

The question was so direct, and I am sad to say, that I didn't have any answers off the top of my head. I stared at a blank page for an entire day of the retreat. I savored the question and longed to be a woman who could answer it easily. I had been so consumed by loving my child and dealing with a hateful, bitter, resentful narcissistic ex, that I didn't know what I needed or wanted. I didn't practice self-love. It never occurred to me to be self-loving as I went through the horror of raising a special needs child with a narc while fighting a legal battle, rigged in his favor because of money.

> **"Where did I go? Did I drown? Did I evaporate?
> Did I quit being me? Did I quit on myself?"**
> *—a journal entry*

I closed my eyes and tried to remember what it was like before the narcissist relationship. What did I use to love to do? It was all so long ago that I had completely forgotten. It took me a while to list some things. I felt guilty even writing them down, never mind secretly wishing for them, even if this was a self-worth exercise. It pained me to write them down because they all cost money, and I used all my money on my child and legal fees, fighting a never-ending court battle. When I read the list, it seemed like a far-fetched fantasy that I didn't have time to even entertain in my mind. The items I listed were like wishful thoughts, so delicate and temporary— like a floating soap bubble that would pop, and leave me with the reality of my beaten-down life that would quickly splatter in my face and sting my eyes. I had very little time to practice self-love while trying to love my daughter and hate the narc.

> **"In order for me to heal my broken life and self . . . I need to
> find the love, feel the love, see the love, and be the love."**
> *—a journal entry*

The weekend was wonderful and moving. It was full of music and meaningful lyrical songs. The songs were all sing-along style, like mantras, and it was very healing to participate in singing those affirmations—very much like a salve for my soul. I still play them when I need a lift. I found some self-love in my heart that weekend, and wept tears of joy in the front row just to feel loved, whole, safe, supported, and alive as a woman, and as a mother. Attending this retreat was an esteemable act, and I was so glad that I fought off the guilt of asking for an overnight babysitter to be able to go.

> **"Note to self: there is tremendous value
> in getting away from one's life!"**
> *—a journal entry*

The weekend renewed my spirits and helped me turn my focus back onto myself. I finally had the opportunity to experience what it was like to be me again—full of hope, dancing to music, talking to other women about what really matters, hearing inspirational stories of overcoming adversity, singing joyfully, and experiencing something new. Being a single, low-income mother for all those years, battling to keep my child safe from a narc, was exhausting, demoralizing, all-consuming, and yet, still a necessity. I needed the break. I needed a soul vacation to come back to myself.

> **"The loving of myself is the ultimate win."**
> —*a journal entry*

I think it was the music and the magic of that weekend that really touched a core part of me. I realized that when something got in that deep, I carried it in my heart forever. Even though I was on a tight budget, I realized the enormous value of the affirmation songs, and purchased some CDs to take home with me to remind me of just what state I want to be in. I discovered that music held the ability to help me instantly shift out of the despair of it all. It helped me remember my innocence, a time before the narc, when I loved people freely, and never experienced the kind of selfishness and cruelty that I now endured for years on the back end of cruel narcissistic love.

> **"No one is going to love me, but me."**
> —*a journal entry*

The weekend opened me up to sharing all my thoughts and feelings with my close friends that I felt safe with. I confessed to a friend that if I really put myself first, I would live out my dream of moving to Hawaii and live out a good life, leaving it all behind. I also confessed something else that was hard to settle inside myself. I reflected on my life, and the one thing that I could see that I did wrong in my life was not live more selfishly. Looking back in review of my life . . . I lived to give to others, never myself. It was freeing to admit that I lived my life too much for others, and given the choice, I would have lived more for myself. I carried my regrets in and out of court.

> **"Love is so beautiful. Hate is so ugly. But I realize now that it's okay to hate evil. However, love will carry me the entire way."**
> —*a journal entry*

Working For vs Working Against

There came a time when I realized that I was so focused on hating the narc and what he had done, that there wasn't much room for any love in my brain—or life. I had allowed the narc to zap the beauty and joy right out of life. If I wanted to raise my child in love, I would have to maintain a loving home, environment, and behavior. I knew that I was the only one capable of this, and it would take work. I was finally willing to accept this new job of self-love. It meant learning to work for myself, instead of against the narc. I had plenty of on-the-job training in learning how to love myself again. Self-love became my solution.

> "I win when I love me."
> —a journal entry

Training vs Trying

So, there I was in my forties, trying to protect my daughter and wanting to love myself at the same time. I was attempting this difficult task with all my fears attached to me like a heavy sack of stones weighing me down. I didn't realize that I could swap out the word "trying" and substitute in the word "training" to make a huge emotional difference. A seasoned therapist threw out this suggestion to me, and at that time, it felt like a life raft thrown at me while I was drowning in my sorrow. He mentioned the option to give up "trying" and go into a type of "training mode." Trying certainly felt heavy, and all my attempts felt useless with a disordered personality like a narc. I felt like I was being swallowed up in a big sea, swimming against the strong oppositional ocean current of a narc, and losing all my energy by aimlessly paddling and kicking. I was trying to co-parent with a narc, I was trying to communicate with a narc, I was trying to get some cooperation from a narc . . . sure, I was trying, but my attempts were completely unsuccessful. Actually, all my efforts were later used against me in a trial.

That small comment became a huge turning point for me. I made the shift in my perspective, and it lined me up for more growth and the attainment of new skills. From that point forward, I decided that I was in training to be able to communicate with a narc in co-parenting, because I was trying and getting nowhere. I began training to confront him on things that concerned me. I began training to handle his allegations and deflections better by naming them clearly and concisely and sticking to the topic. I was in training to be more business-like with him and eliminate the personal elements. I learned to throw the ball back into his court, so to speak, by asking him why he can't stick to the topic of raising our daughter. Also, I began training for another round of Family Court, because it was inevitable.

> "I used to ask myself, how do I avoid court? Now I ask myself, how do I use it? This is a fundamental change/shift in my thinking."
> —a journal entry

When I considered it just practice and training in the art of co-parenting with a toxic person, it felt more doable. I learned to write as if a court liaison were reading my messages to the narc, and considered how they would be viewed. I wrote for myself, and for them. I was able to say things more clearly and get more skilled, even though I wasn't able to get the cooperation I wanted. I was able to message him about how he was being uncooperative and be upfront about the situations as they happened. I stopped waiting for cooperation from him. I was getting better at communication, and to my astonishment, he—the one who usually could rant and twist the conversation—grew silent. I had found my voice!

> **"I can look back now and see that I loved myself very little. I was so concerned with getting his love for basic survival. Why did I think I needed him to survive? Just because he said so? Oh, how I was trained to go against myself!"**
> *—a journal entry*

After that woman's retreat, after a fifteen-year-long relationship with a narc, and a decade-long court battle, I was trying to love myself. This became my new frontier—training to love myself. I began exploring ways to do this, and I put myself into a kind of self-training program. I often had to wear many hats to survive narcissistic abuse. I had to become my own therapist, my own legal counsel, and my own life coach to cheer myself on. I became my own teacher and guru.

I may have never gotten the narc to cooperate, but I learned the vocabulary I needed to be more self-respecting.

> **"I am done with you because I choose me."**
> *—a journal entry*

I trained myself to consistently do things that brought me a sense of love, happiness, and comfort. I routinely read books about love, happiness, and positive thinking. I watched movies that I loved that had a positive message and happy ending. I played with young children and had fun. I listened to sermons and TED talks about love. I immersed myself in love. I made sure that I was around loving people, doing loving things. When love was everywhere in my life, it blocked out the damaging effects of hate—both his and mine. Making a deliberate, conscious choice to crowd out my despair and fear with love was the healthiest thing that I could do for myself. The year that I fell ill, I researched what would help me heal. Experts from neuroscientists to psychologists to preachers all pointed in the direction of love. Choose love.

The Power in Self-Love

I think the most heartbreaking part of my situation was not that my love couldn't fix my ex's major personality dysfunction, nor that my love couldn't get him to stop drinking, nor that my love couldn't cure my daughter's condition . . . it was that I didn't love myself well enough.

Still, I knew deep down that love is very powerful. I gained the energy I needed with self-love. Self-love became the fuel I needed to keep going and keep loving my child. With self-love, I became a better friend to myself. As I became a more astute student of self-love, I was learning to manage my energy better. My power needed to be channeled in the right direction. I began to look at what cost me power, how to get power, and what power really mattered in the grand scheme of things. I wanted to make better choices about where I put my love, who I choose to love, and how I loved myself.

The Story of the Two Wolves

I was reminded of the old Native American story about the two wolves. I first heard this story on another retreat, and it left a memorable mental image. The presenter showed us a poster of an Indian profile with a white wolf and a black wolf merging in the background. The white wolf symbolized all that was good, pure, and loving. The black wolf stood for all that was bad, evil, and hateful. The story is about how every day we make the choice of which one to feed. As you would expect, the one that grows the most powerful is the one that is fed. Right then and there, I had to decide to feed my self-love, and not continue to feed my hatred towards the narc.

> **"I now deem every self-loving act a personal win."**
> —*a journal entry*

Establish Self-Rule #4 = Keep The Focus on Love (Do whatever you need to do to keep a reminder about what's most important. Fill your mind, home, and life with love. If you get side-tracked with bitterness and resentment, pull yourself back and into love. Go where you feel love, and be with people who are loving. You may need to build a new life for yourself - one that is a container of love for you to heal and thrive in. Love your children, in any way that you can - even if it's praying for them daily. Find ways to give and receive love.)

Self-Reflection Questions:

- What do you love about your child/children?
- What do you love about life?
- What can you read, watch, or do that is centered around love?
- What is something self-loving that you can do today?
- Weekly?
- Monthly?

Self-Rule #5

CONTINUE HEALING

"Healing will forever be the most important part of my life."
—*a journal entry*

The professional psychological community has finally recognized narcissistic abuse victims as having a unique, documentable, identifiable, and real condition. The pain was certainly insidious, and the type of pain is very specific to this type of abuse. This results in Narcissistic Abuse Syndrome; a very hard to get over, powerful condition. To create this horrible disorder in the victim, the narc purposely plants dark seeds in the target's mind. Actually, they are more like wiggly worms or parasites. When these words worm their way into the foundations of the target's mind, the mind becomes infected in a way that is difficult to explain. You only have to watch the movie Gaslight to know. People generally cringe when they see the absolute terror of the victims.

"My healing is crucial for continued survival."
—*a journal entry*

I need to heal from that parasitic relationship with the narc and detox all the worms in my mind. I felt sucked dry of my life and blood by him. It was like I had just spent fifteen years with an energy vampire, and eight years hiding in an attempt to escape. Sadly, my escape wasn't soon enough as I ended up pregnant on the way out of the dungeon. Unfortunately, my future would be forever scarred, because I was running away with shackles. Now, I am always having to keep a safe distance away and always make sure others are surrounding me in the light of day, or I could be targeted and bitten, and possibly infected again!

> "I must put caution tape over every area the narc is
> to remember to stay away from his toxicity."
> —*a journal entry*

Abuse by Proxy Is Real

The abuse was so subtle, yet cut so deep. At first, I didn't even know I was being abused by him. Exchanging our child because of shared custody began to get creepy and hostile—that's when I sought help. In that relationship, I let the snide remarks about me roll off my back, thinking that it wasn't getting to me, but it chiseled away at my soul like toxic, acidic rainwater and eventually made me weak just standing near the source... him. When I felt like the court was being used as a weapon to punish me for leaving him, I realized that I was being abused in a new way. The term was called "abuse by proxy," and it is effective on a victim, too. I sought the services of a local domestic violence agency to understand what was happening to me and how to make the abuse stop. Unfortunately, we could only identify it, but we were unable to stop that type of abuse. My DV worker often came to my court appearances to just sit and watch the abuse take place.

> "The abuse had different levels, so my
> healing will be on different levels, too."
> —*a journal entry*

Since I was the mother of our child, and yet leaving the narc, I was brutally criticized, condemned, scapegoated, persecuted, and accused of the most horrific things. My attorney once commented that this was a modern-day "witch hunt." The narc complained about me to every professional so that they either quit, called Child Protective Services on me, or showed up to testify against me. I learned the tactics of a narc first hand. I found out what a flying monkey was by having one come after me on his behalf. I experienced his ability to create minions, and watched them do his dirty work. I saw him pay thousands of dollars to get the most greedy, corrupt, unethical attorney to represent him, one that would stop at nothing to win. His attorney happily billed everything she could by extending the battle for years, and refusing to meet in a four-way and negotiate. No one could think about our child while they were so concerned about attacking me. My ex was an expert on shifting blame, deflecting, and sending an innocent to slaughter. Even though I was aware of what was happening, I could do nothing to stop it. It was like standing in a gas chamber while they slowly turned on the gas. I could feel the deadly air coming each time he opened his mouth, and in court, I had to stand there silent, still, and poised.

"It's vital that I heal so I can remain standing."
—a journal entry

The nightmares and inability to sleep, haunted me for years. I did my best to focus on my child and me——and keep him in a box in my mind. It was wonderful to have him out of sight and protection orders in place, but I knew how angry he was from all the boundaries I had erected. I was afraid of his mental state. I was afraid of his retaliation. I could only hold on to what I had and wait for a battle. I was so traumatized by the whole legal war with the narc that I needed decades of healing. I had lost faith in the justice system. I especially lost faith in the ethicality of court systems. They were unable to detect narcissism in a toxic parent. In my case, the guardian ad litem voted for him. It couldn't have been more backward.

"They say that wherever there is the presence of pain, there is a need for healing. I am in so much pain, I will need so much healing."
—a journal entry

The abuse lasted years, and I endured it so that my child could be sheltered and protected under the law. I stuck my neck out for her by getting her the Early Intervention services she needed. Getting help for her meant getting attacked because the narc disagreed with every claim I made while I advocated for the legitimate needs of our child. The narc insisted our child was perfect, even though she struggled socially, physically, and otherwise. He couldn't handle the truth. He probably couldn't even see her struggle, because he was only looking at himself. The reason for him presenting such positive statements to professionals was because he knew it made him look good. Simply put, he was selfish.

I was ruthlessly attacked for all the help I got her. Instead of commending me for how well she was doing, they blamed me for diagnoses that were done at age two, and later revised. They shifted everyone's focus and claimed that all the help that I got her, actually was harmful. They were insane in insisting that I was the cause of all my child's problems. They tried to make the case that, because I pointed out her needs, that I was the problem. Nope.

Being on the "receiving end" of all the blame was tough. Even though I knew the truth—I was living a hellish experience as a parent who just wanted to help her struggling kid. I did my best, even though they criticized me. I went ahead with getting her help, even though the narc claimed she didn't need it. I did the right thing, and was a living martyr. Most mothers in these types of situations are. We love our children and will die for them. My ex killed my life.

> **"There are parts of me that have had to lay dormant for years to survive raising a child on my own. There are so many parts of me that need my nurturing to come back to life. I will have to resurrect myself."**
> *—a journal entry*

I was a legally battered woman. Even though his cheating was always hidden with lies of omission, I was outright sucker-punched, day after day, behind the scenes to professionals. It was a tactic called a smear campaign. The character defamation worked to a large extent. When he reverted to the "poisoning the well" tactic, I was on guard and trying to head him off at every pass. That proved too difficult and required all my daily mental energy. I had to cut my losses and walk away. Playing was not only hurtful, but felt deadly. During that time period, my life was dead and devoid of any joy. It was a living landmine.

> **"I need to function."**
> *—a journal entry*

To really instill fear, he would remark about how many guns he owned at every pediatrician's office, only to hear the doctor ask if they are locked up in a safe. Bringing it up felt purposeful and planted. He had an agenda to keep me afraid. I had to face my fears.

I learned that the main weapon a narc uses is the target's fears. I learned that the primary way the narcissistic parent wins is by destabilizing the target. It was paramount that I heal and remain stable to care for my child. I needed to remain sane.

> **"How do I care for myself? How do I care for my energy? I need my own TLC."**
> *—a journal entry*

I needed a long rehabilitation program to heal. I had to let go of my child for five days in a row with the new plan, so I used it to detach from both of their problems. Without either one in my apartment, I was free from all the disorders and chronic complaining. I was able to breathe my own breaths for myself, and not live for the sole purpose of helping another put on their oxygen mask.

> "I am taking a path to a healed life."
> —*a journal entry*

Investing in my Healing Journey

I needed to heal from the torture and the fear. As part of my self-care routine, I go to counseling. I already had a support system in place to keep me standing for as long as I did through the decade of court. I had a private therapist, a domestic violence counselor, a Twelve-Step recovery program of Al-Anon with weekly meetings with a solid home group, an amazing program sponsor who attends five meets per week, a weekly Nonviolent Communication Group, a monthly Women of Spirit Group, sermons from two different local churches for spiritual support, and many conscious and educated friends. Even more so, I had done specific energy healing certifications, shamanic training about finding our power, and other self-help/empowerment trainings. I blended them all. I took whatever nugget any healing modality provided, and added it to my coping tools.

> **"Note to self: The narcs #1 tactic for winning the children is to destabilize the target. They seem to know that messing with mom's mind is a way to make her crazy, then be able to call her crazy. A narc's next move is to point the finger, make a false accusation, and watch her, the target, unravel—then claim victory. Advice to self: Stay stable!"**
> —*a journal entry*

However, the most helpful things were the healings that were specific to narcissistic abuse. Narcissistic Abuse Syndrome is a very specific problem, with a very unhappy outcome for the psychologically battered victims. Other helpful resources were online videos describing the ins and outs of narcissism. Education on the topic helped me understand why he wanted to continue to haunt me. It wasn't personal, it was just who he was.

> "I know that a healthy mom is a better parent. And a healed parent is the best parent. I vow to evolve into a healthy person for her—whatever it takes!"
> —*a journal entry*

I had to invest in my healing programs. I had to be part of online communities that were specifically for narcissistic abuse victims. They knew all too well what I was going through, and could explain it better than I could. The sense of community was so important. I corresponded by email with those women, and they provided me resources in the form of blog articles explaining specific topics. That education on narcissism was incredibly valuable. Still, I had no way to fix him, or my problem. Instead, I had to turn to healing the best I could on my days off from parenting.

Holy Trouble and Spiritual Healing

In my desperation, I also sought out spiritual healing to recover from the abuse. It had certainly drained my spirit to be under attack. My soul was weary and bruised. I learned to pray and lean on a Higher Power for support. I was willing to try any remedy to heal— New-age or Old Testament. Oftentimes, I felt like my ex was pure evil, and when I read the Bible, I saw that they often had to cast out demons from people as a natural course of action for those afflicted with jealousy, rage, and mental illness. If only!

While I couldn't cast out a demon, I could call for help with my healing process. I kept an open mind and tried many healing programs, became part of many narcissistic abuse recovery groups, and wrote my story for all to read and see. Even though I had lost, I was on my road back to health and happiness without the narc, and with a new focus. When my child was with her father, I learned to be grateful for my "healing time." Gratitude was a quick cure for some of my pain.

> **"I need to heal at the deepest level. I need to heal at the "I-love-me- level." It's such a deeper level than I even have a term for. I need to heal at my core."**
> *—a journal entry*

When I focused on my healing as my priority, I felt energy pour into me, instead of out onto all the problems the narc created. I took to healing as my full-time job. I blended all the therapies and used whatever was helpful. I found that the most helpful thing was hearing how other women survived it, and now have grown children.

I decided if they could withstand a narc and grow old, so can I. In writing my story, I hope to help someone searching for the answers like I was.

> **"Healing is where my answer is. I repeat: Healing is the answer."**
> *—a journal entry*

Establish Self-Rule #5 = Continue Healing. (Focus on your healing and prioritize your healing. You will need lots of ongoing healing to process the attacks, lies, and other forms of narcissistic abuse —especially any co-parenting abuse/post-separation abuse. Establish a healing plan for yourself. Whether this is therapy, support groups, programs, etc. Do what works for you. Combine things to address your mind, body, spirit, and soul.)

Self-Reflection Questions:

- What can you do to heal?
- What type of healing have you tried that works?
- What type of healing would you like to try?
- What needs healing in your life?
- What needs healing in your mind?
- Body?
- Spirit?

Self-Rule #6

DO EACH THING AS IT COMES

> **"My situation will not be solved, the narc will continue to persist, so how do I pace myself?"**
> *—a journal entry*

The level of anxiety that I suffered out of fear of what the narcissist would do next is beyond what I can convey. To effectively deal with all the crises, I had to become like a robot and learn simply to do each thing as it came. I had to be unemotional and just process the data and requests, and only do whatever was needed at the time.

To turn into a walking, functioning, robotic mother who followed legal commands was my best strategy, because my instincts were screaming, "This father is toxic and endangering the health and safety of the child!" However, following my reactionary maternal instincts did very little to protect her since there were family systems in place with their own specific protocols and standards. I was no longer in charge.

> **"We all failed her. All I can tell myself is that I know that I tried."**
> *—a journal entry*

The Many Failures of Society

Child Protective Services screened out many of my complaints and fears because they didn't meet the level of abuse or neglect required to initiate an investigation. All my fearful calls into authorities or agencies set up to protect children were then used against me at trial. Some of the incidents were clearly harmful to the child, but when the agency examined the nature of the harm, they didn't have the necessary resources to care about things such as feeding the child food that she might be allergic to. They had more dangerous situations to deal with and limited resources to run on. As much as I hated that they couldn't help me, I understood. There was very little anyone could do about the small amounts of harm the narc dished out daily.

> **"My horrible case was the perfect storm of my lawyer's incompetence, his lawyers' unethical save, and the narc's tactics of triangulation, lying, finger-pointing, smearing, hiring minions, and recruiting of a professional flying monkey. I only wish I told myself to hire better representation, even if it meant taking out a loan for a legal retainer. I wish I had done that now. It would have been a good investment. I was just too scared at the time. I was being so attacked. It felt like being tried as a criminal in Family Court. All I was guilty of was being a loving mom."**
> *—a journal entry*

When the legal system also began to fail to protect my child, I was at a loss. Everything in my body was afraid for her to be with him unsupervised. I knew that deep down, even his parents were fearful for her, though they would never admit it because they were so focused on protecting their son from going to jail. I saw how a narc could easily appeal to the sympathy of others when they got themselves in trouble. Crying and complaining to his parents, pointing out the other parent—me—as the "bad guy," and justifying actions or inactions are clever and very effective tactics narcs use. I always had to keep in mind that I, too, fell for all of this once upon a time.

> **"I have to remind myself that it's not all my fault!"**
> *—a journal entry*

In a variety of ways, the people, the agencies, and the legal system all failed to protect our child from the narc's abuse. I even failed to hire an adequate attorney for this type of complicated legal battle. While with her dad, she was subjected to all kinds of harm, from bug bites all over her body, to emotional abuse. It's entirely painful for me to even witness this, being an empath.

> **"Empaths are drawn to narcs, and narcs are drawn to empaths. It goes both ways, but I feel used. Wait, I was used. The narc knew that I would clean up all these messes and raise the children—that's why he hooked me in the first place."**
> *—a journal entry*

I realized that the narc plays in the "gray area" where he is least likely to get called out or caught—where it is very effective just to explain a story that appeals to the listener to divert blame and responsibility. I had to learn to tolerate witnessing the abuse with my hands figuratively tied behind my back and duct tape over my mouth. It was a nightmare playing out in the daytime, and there was little that I could do for her. I found myself routinely putting Band-Aids on her cuts, Neosporin on her gashes, anti-itch cream on all her bug bites, giving her gas pain relief drops for her upset stomachs due to too much lactose, diaper rash cream on all her serious painful rashes, ice packs for all her swelling, rushing to get antibiotics for ticks pulled off of her, and giving Tylenol at 2 a.m. for her headaches. I suffered right alongside her. I barely got any sleep so that she could.

> **"I am so full of angry, red hot rage that if I were an actual momma bear, I would claw his eyes out and leave him for dead. No animal can tolerate their baby being hurt."**
> —*a journal entry*

The few times that injuries rose to the level of filing a formal complaint, I acted with courage. However, even though professionals reported the allegations and corroborated the evidence, I think the charm and child-coaching tactics of the narc were all too powerful for amateurs. I quickly realized that a better detection system needed to be in place for children. Just because a child doesn't repeat the same disturbing sentence she said to therapists in a formal investigative interview doesn't mean bad things didn't happen to her that were completely inappropriate. There needs to be a better system.

> **"There is no way that a human being can give their most valuable, vulnerable prized possession to an enemy and be okay with that. A person does not hand the thing they love the most to a dangerous enemy and leave it unprotected. What is wrong with the court system!? Do they understand human beings at all? Do they know anything about maternal instincts?**
> —*a journal entry*

Currently, this is the sad, inept state of the system that I experienced. Incidents have to be blatant and provable, which is hardly ever the case with a clever narc. In my view, the system utterly failed my child, though I was still grateful to have a place to call and made several reports. My complaints at least let the narc know that I would act and that he had to either behave or get reported.

Unfortunately, all the reports were used against me in trial and painted me as an overbearing, overprotective, reactionary, unstable mother. I knew the truth as they listed all the calls that I made to the authorities, trying to protect my child. At my trial, only my attorney could speak for me; all I could do was sit there in silence, sad that no one took the reports seriously.

In hindsight, my therapist told me that if I didn't make the calls, then the situation would have escalated to the point where he was trying to steal custody and order the judge to have me on supervised visitation. However, I had to explain to her that the situation wasn't friendly or pleasant, even before my formally-filed complaints. Actually, it was horrendous. I was being alienated and completely left in the dark about where she was sleeping or staying during his visits.

I have often looked back at my decision to report what I believed to be inappropriate sexual contact, and I still believe that I made the right call in reporting it right away. The courage it took for me to make that report sent a shockwave through his family. They in turn, rallied around him, helping him parent our child. After I made that brave and bold report, she enjoyed four years of sleeping at her grandparents—his parents. I cannot regret how that changed her circumstances, significantly. It was a "win" for her, but a harmful mark on me as a mom when it came to the trial.

By being in such a hyper state of awareness and on alert, I was feeling the effects of adrenal fatigue. I was always afraid for her life whenever she spent time with the narc. After the unfavorable ruling, I had to talk myself down from the ledge of my fear by telling myself that his parents are closely watching both her and him now. Or at the least, he will have to answer to both his lawyer and a judge if something truly terrible happened, because he certainly wouldn't answer to me. To say that he had real issues with authority is an understatement—he didn't respect authority.

I was so dismayed when my first and second attorney informed me that our case would likely be in and out of court for the duration of our child's life. In my denial, I falsely believed that someday this would settle, and the narc would come to his senses and cooperate.

The day I finally admitted and acknowledged that this fantasy was not to be my reality was the day I stopped fearing court. I, instead, looked to use it to our child's advantage. If I had lost control of him, if his parents had lost control of him, if his attorney's advice didn't matter to him, then it was up to the judge to steer him. That became my winning mindset. No more hoping that he would turn into a nice guy or do the right thing!

I had to begin to simplify things into the present moment, because my fears of the future would overwhelm me. Mentally, I could connect the dots and add up the past to see the projected extent of the damage a narc could do to our child. I was very concerned for her well-being. I knew that the impact of a cold, uncaring, self-centered parent was detrimental.

In my childhood, I had a father somewhere on the narcissistic spectrum. I disapproved of his behavior, as well. I vowed to never leave my child alone or unattended with him. I also saw his mother display narcissistic tendencies, as well. I saw the effects of narcissistic abuse on children in both me and my ex. I also saw how his preaching his philosophies and monologues were seeping into our child's mind. The additional time with him was becoming apparent in her psyche.

On many occasions, he said disparaging words to our child, and I would later hear the same comments coming out of her mouth. I had to let her know that they were not kind, nor appropriate. I did my best to help her understand that this was not okay, while also trying not to make her feel bad for hearing them in the first place. This was always so difficult to handle well. Whenever she realized he was doing something wrong or bad, she felt shame, too. The narc was her dad, and children identify with their parents.

For a child, I realized that it was incredibly challenging to separate him from herself and have a conversation about correct thinking or appropriate behavior, but I still felt like the truth had to be said to her, otherwise, she would have been made to believe morally wrong things. I spent hours trying to find the words to convey a message that wouldn't hurt her feelings.

It was to my relief when she told me how his mother was yelling at him for doing inappropriate things to her, or neglecting her needs. It was refreshing to hear her grandfather stepped up to intervene on her behalf from time to time, too. This all took place on his parenting time, and I was out of reach and left entirely in the dark about what was happening. It helped me to know that I wasn't the only one concerned about her well-being whenever she was in his care. My fears were legitimate.

At times, for comfort, I would tell myself that if something happened to her, it would be his parents' fault. I was sick of feeling overly responsible. I had to be so overly responsible because the narc lacked responsibility. I reasoned with myself that since she is their only grandchild, and they want to enable their son, then they need to either step up or lose her. I also told myself that if they all want to take the stand to support him at the trial, then if something terrible happens to her, they are the reason behind it. I did my best, but it was five-against-one.

That was the ultimate "letting go" point for me. I had to let go of her life and turn it over to him, his family, and society. When I lost my legal rights, it felt like I had lost my ability to single-handedly keep her alive and healthy. It was a harrowing reality to face. I wished that she was at least sixteen, because then I could bear the loss, but not with her being only eight-years-old. She was too terrified to speak up to her dad about anything, and I stopped helping her try to do so since every effort backfired on us. She had to cope in her own way to survive him.

I had to watch my little girl shut down and internalize all her true feelings and needs while in his care, only to come back to me wailing and crying hysterically about anything and everything. I understood that I was her safe person, and she needed to get it all out. I worked hard on myself to hold a safe space for her. I learned not to try to "fix" it, but just to listen and validate her experiences. I had to learn to believe in her abilities to cope.

Considering how each time the narc neglected her, she would become injured, I had to learn not to create "mountains out of molehills." If she was in one piece when I got her back, I was thankful. I had to keep it very simple in my mind to withstand the continued problems that arose. I had to focus on the fact that she was currently alive and breathing. I had to remember how much she had already survived, and use that as strength for the next time.

However, I knew that the trauma was building up in her. I knew that with her extreme separation anxiety, and the courts taking her away from her mother and handing her to a father who lacked parenting abilities, was what was causing her a lot of pain. Then I had to face all that was being handed back to me. She would get UTI's from dirty diapers, rashes from foods she was allergic to, gas pains from the dairy that would keep her up crying all night, headaches from concussions, injuries from outings, bug bites from being outdoors, and the list goes on and on.

I had to bear witness to all of her pain, and all I could do was be sad to have to see it. It was infuriating when pediatricians took his side, saying that these were all normal childhood issues.

Good friends reminded me that I couldn't shelter or protect her from everything in life. They told me that kids would naturally get hurt without having to blame the other parent. I tried to reason with myself every time I received her back from her dad in bad shape. People tried to help by telling me that kids are resilient and that they can bounce back. I had to hang onto every positive, reassuring, calming statement from any parent, just to get through the years of not co-parenting with the narc. She was surviving her childhood, and so was I.

I had to face everything one day at a time. I had to keep it simple. I had to stick to the day just to have enough energy for tomorrow. I had to reassure myself. I had to validate my concerns and bring them to the attention of my new attorney. I had to continue advocating for her needs in any way possible that wasn't harming my case. It was a very tricky and extremely complicated way to parent and protect a child; however, it was what I had to do.

When things got challenging for me to handle emotionally, I would list the advantages that she had over starving children in other parts of the world. This sometimes helped me to keep our problems in perspective. Here's what I listen for perspective:

1. She wasn't starving.
2. She had healthcare and vaccinations.
3. She had a mom and a dad, and she wasn't an unfortunate orphan.
4. The year is 2020 and not 1818, which has so many advantages for children.
5. She had a home and wasn't homeless.
6. She had free schooling and many advantages from the educational system.
7. There is a family court system and laws in place.
8. She was in a small, safe town with both sets of grandparents living.
9. She had her good health; she wasn't a kid dying from cancer.
10. She had a mother who was educated and aware. A mother who loved her, and who would help her overcome things, and would always be there for her. She had me.

I said all these things to my worried, frazzled mind. Sometimes I said them aloud to affirm what she did have and to keep myself thinking positive thoughts. It was an effective coping mechanism.

My new way of dealing with things had me becoming very robotic to where I would not react without careful consideration. I had to make myself very intentional and deliberate in dealing with the narc. I could not be my loving, caring self with him, as that particular people-pleasing character trait of mine was always used to his advantage.

I had to be business-like in all my correspondence with him, to follow the court orders, and issue consequences like the authorities would do anytime he was in contempt of the agreement. I had to adopt a new way of dealing with the narc. I executed all of my patience, took countless pictures, confronted him on OFW, and planned to use the legal avenue just like he did to me. It was the only way I could see it working, because things weren't working. So I did each thing as it came. It was one day at a time, and one problem at a time.

Establish Self-Rule #8 = Do Each Thing As it Comes (safeguard against any overwhelm, by having a plan to tackle each obstacle, threat, and problem as they arise—rather than cave into fear and worry. Having a support team ready to catch you from anything triggering can be key to quickly moving on from any trauma, drama, and chaos the narcissist drums up.)

Self-Reflection Questions:x

- What do you have to do right at this moment?
- What do you have to do today to keep your life running?
- How can you keep it simple?
- What are the immediate needs of your child/children?
- What are your immediate needs?
- How can you meet them more easily?

Self-Rule #7

WRITE AND SHARE

> **"As long as I am writing it all down, I am winning clarity. And other's win my testimony."**
> —*a journal entry*

Family Court felt like a concentration camp. It was the place I was being held while they systematically stripped me of my dignity and power. And the narc was all about power. That's ultimately what he wanted to steal from me. It was "the thing" he was after. I felt like I didn't have much power after losing custody, but I was determined to use whatever power I had to warn other women. After making so many mistakes, I felt like I had so much wisdom locked up inside of me, that it might be a treasure trove to another struggling mother—even if it just provided much-needed emotional support.

> **"In my silence, I see what is happening. In my silence, I write, which is a form of speaking up, even if I am the only one who is listening."**
> —*a journal entry*

One day, about halfway through writing this book, I realized that the main reason I was writing so frantically after my legal loss was because I was actively grieving. My grief was so gut-wrenching that I had to throw myself into a project or risk getting consumed by depression. Every word I typed after the judge's order felt like a teardrop falling from my face and onto my fingers. Writing often felt like Anne Frank's diary. I was documenting my journey, trying to make sense of it all while attempting to live a normal, healthy life behind the walls and out of view from the narc.

> *"I have realized that I am not just writing for healing, but because I am sorely grieving."*
> —*a journal entry*

I felt compelled to write for many reasons, with some of the main ones being: 1) to document everything the narc was doing, 2) to encourage myself—in a daily private journal—to keep going, 3) to heal, 4) to serve others and attempt to help other mothers going through similar horrors, and 5) to grieve.

The Value of a Daily Journal

> *"Writing validates my reality. I don't need anyone else's approval."*
> —*a journal entry*

Just like that famous diary of Anne Frank, I found journaling to be life-saving. I had to use my journaling time to get in touch with my feelings and to recap the lessons learned. Being that no failure was just failure, there was always a valuable lesson to be learned. To survive a narc, I had to live "out of sight" of the enemy. It was horrible stress to endure, but what was worse was being on his radar and in his scope.

It felt like I could tell my whole story—the good, the bad, and the ugly—in a journal without anyone editing it or criticizing my thoughts and feelings. This was crucial for me to learn to trust myself, be there for myself, and to "back" myself. Writing a journal was a daily dose of self-approval and self-validation. My experience was horrible, traumatic, and real. Plus, I had to live out my day-to-day life, pay the bills, and do the laundry all while showing up to each court appearance.

Listing Wins and Gratitudes

There was one other important reason that I wrote privately, especially at the end of the day—it was to list my wins and my gratitudes. If I fell into a deep sadness, I would force myself to list everything that I was grateful for. I wrote down everything—from the pillow on my bed, my half-time with my child, and even the food on my refrigerator shelves. The gratitude list had a way of instantly shifting my thoughts and my mood.

Maintaining a Good Mood, Regardless

I knew that how I thought about everything in my life would influence my experience. I also knew that how I behaved as a person would impact my daughter. The one thing that I could control was my mood, so long as I got control of my thoughts. I wanted my child to have a mother who was positive, upbeat, happy, and joyful. I wanted to be that for her so she could have some of these good qualities, too. I made having a good mood my daily goal.

> "I can't give into depression because it will consume me and haunt my child. I still need to grieve and cry, though. I have to find a way to reserve that time with someone safe who will listen to my woes, but not allow me to stay there. I want her to have a happy childhood—no matter my pain."
> —*a journal entry*

Writing to Clear Away the Pain and Process It

Writing was a cathartic experience for me. I felt relief every time I shared a tattered piece of my tragic story. It was so therapeutic that on the days I didn't have my daughter, I would write and write. I spent hours writing. It was how I made it through the early months of my loss without crying every five minutes. I felt like I could write and refresh myself spiritually on the pages of truth. It not only cleared the cobwebs of my mind and provided me insight, but it also gave me hope. I discovered that writing was a form of self-generated hope.

> "As long as I am alive, here, and stable—my child is winning."
> —*a journal entry*

I felt like if I could become very clear on the page about the tactics of the narc, I would stay level-headed during the co-parenting battles with him. I found this to be true since staying aware and sharp was very similar to having all your guns ready for battle. My writing was a very effective tool in many ways. I was advised by several legal professionals that, in my unfortunate case, the battles would be unending. I had to accept this reality.

I decided that if I had to endure it, then I would document this journey. I not only documented on OFW for future legal use, but I also documented everything that I found helpful for coping, and wanted to share this information with other mothers, and maybe even fathers, dealing with a narc as a co-parent.

Fathers, Too!

I had certainly seen emotionally crippled men attempt to recover from divorcing narcissistic women, only to have their children alienated from them and all their finances dried up. I can still see their discouraged faces at the Twelve-Step support group meetings I attended. When they shared how their ex wanted it all and was never happy, it was my first clue that these men were dealing with narcs. I felt sorry for these men. I knew them to be good, loyal, hard-working, and loving guys. This just so happens to be precisely what a narc looks for! I saw myself in them and saw how much the narcissistic women alienated the children from these great dads.

Over the years of attending those meetings, it was so sad to watch these men grieve. Now, I was that person. I was a mother who was being alienated and turning broke by the legal billable hour.

> *"To be able to recognize the patterns is to be immune from relapse."*
> —*a journal entry*

Writing to Warn!

My purpose for publishing my writing is my hope that a mother will read my book and know that she is not alone. That someday, I will receive emails or see reviews on Amazon saying that my book helped to save a life. I so desperately want women to be forewarned about this common pattern of narcs stealing children and using the court system as a form of abuse by proxy. I want women to know that playing defense is a way for them to continue feeling threatened and attacked. I want women to be empowered and knowledgeable so that they can maintain their rights to their children.

> *"To remember what happened and to always know what is happening is to be immune from the narc."*
> —*a journal entry*

I will always fondly remember this one woman in her seventies who knew all too well what I was dealing with. She always listened quietly to my story, for she, too, had an ex-husband who stole both her son and her daughter from her through the legal system, using money and the family courts.

Her children were lavished with all that the narc's money could buy, but in reflection, she realized that money couldn't buy the most basic of human needs. Decades ago, she bravely walked away from her abuser, the house, and her children thinking that they would be okay.

She advised me not to stop fighting because her husband did so much psychological damage to her two children, that when they reached their early adulthood, her son died from a drug overdose and her daughter committed suicide.

When I heard that outcome, when I saw the flat, cold truth in her face, I was startled. I felt a form of reality-shock. It helped me realize that just walking away and accepting my losses wasn't the best long-term option for my child. I realized just how psychologically harmful a narc could truly be.

> "I cannot give up, even if it feels like I am losing.
> My child needs me in ways I cannot put into words."
> —*a journal entry*

That mother advised me to stay mentally stable for my child. She told me that her choice to leave the scene—to save her own life— resulted in a horrific outcome. She lamented that she couldn't do better at the time with her being so broken while the narc looked so stable. I knew with every fiber of my being that I was my child's psychological buffer from the narc. I knew she was too young to be blamed, picked apart, and verbally destroyed by his selfishness and lack of concern for her needs.

This is why I chose to remain there, standing in court and getting attacked as a mother while seeking early intervention for her. With the narc's clever diversion tactic, every need she had was blamed on me. Another mother trying to support me through my crisis told me that I have "big shoulders," and that I am an adult and can handle the blame, but my child is too fragile and cannot. I knew this was true. My daughter was crushed by every negative comment aimed at her. She was terrified of her father. She was terrified to show any feelings around her father. She refused to speak up or to have any preference other than his. She was right to employ this coping strategy. That mother left her children at home with a narc to go to work, and he sexually abused them. I listened to every ounce of wisdom she poured out to me.

> "To never go to the hardware store for bread is a win.
> To never go to the narc for sympathy is a victory."
> —*a journal entry*

My Mistakes

The few times I helped my daughter speak up to her father, she got the brunt of his unhappiness and cruelty. It was unhelpful to tell her to confront a well-seasoned, argumentative, arrogant narc in charge of her.

It was like having her walk up to Hitler as a Jew and ask for some sympathy. He wasn't capable. He was mentally ill. The outcome of a conversation with her father was further traumatizing. When I called the narc on her behalf for sympathy, he got angry and hostile. When I asked for his help, cooperation, and consideration for our child, he hung up the phone on us.

All he could contribute to any conversation was his disordered, paranoid, and selfish self. He was a dry well for any type of compassion, sympathy, or empathy. He had none to give, and as every instinctual mother knows, this is a disaster for a young, vulnerable child.

Personally, I never even wanted to see my ex have a pet. He lacked so much concern for others, or the ability to identify and meet another's needs, that it was scary!

> **"Note to self: He is harmful. We must stay away."**
> —*a journal entry*

I learned so much from hearing other people's experiences with narcs. I especially learned a lot from the personal stories of tragedy. I paid close and careful attention to the details. When I heard what went wrong with a narc after a reasonable line of thinking was applied, I immediately made a "note to self" to NEVER try such and such, myself. I underestimated the evil that my ex was capable of.

At the trial, when he allowed his attorney to throw everything damaging at me—from my painful, complicated, and traumatic childbirth experience where he started to break down into tears because he wasn't allowed at the birth, to exploiting my GoFundMe page and my physical disability due to a genetic disorder—I saw that I couldn't put anything past him. He would attempt to win at whatever cost, even if he lacked moral character in doing so. He was corrupt. He had no moral code of honor. Anything and everything would be used against me.

> **"A friend of mine told me that I will 'outgrow not only people, but my problems.' I can only hope."**
> —*a journal entry*

The bottom line is that I was a survivor of a lengthy legal battle with a narc. I came out with half-physical custody retained. I knew that some mothers only ended up with supervised visits with their children. I knew that to walk away would be harmful to my daughter and bury me in terrible guilt. Staying, confronting, fighting, equipping myself, and becoming assertive felt like the right thing to do for us both. Being nice got me in trouble. Being nice is what attracted a narc to me. I had to stop being nice. I had to hold back my core self from someone who wanted to suck my blood.

I had to bring this "vampire" into the light where they shrivel. It was going to take amounts of courage that I didn't yet have to confront him and keep fighting. I even started writing prayers for myself to stay strong. I knew that I gained courage through my connections with others. Connecting with other mothers was so valuable to me.

> **"Writing is what helped me rise up out of my scared, small self."**
> *—a journal entry*

Knowing a few things about history, I knew that I was going to need a "United Nations" type of front to take out/eliminate threats of the clever narc. Many countries had to unite to defeat the Nazis. My attempts at acquiring professionals to see his true colors was only half-successful. I needed another legal strategy and not to focus on the small battles lost due to corruption.

> **"A sense of community is paramount in this situation."**
> *—a journal entry*

During this time, I watched as President Trump wiggled, weaseled, worded, and threatened legal action against anyone daring enough to call his reign mishandled. It felt eerily similar to my life on a smaller scale. The impeachment process didn't work on him. I watched the President hire other slimy, money-hungry worms to cover up things and take an offensive approach. He knew exactly how to escape criticism and blame. With that, he was a pro.

For me, I was dealing with a Trump-Hitler type narc and watched a similar saga play out on national news. When I realized the many striking similarities, I didn't feel so bad about losing in Family Court. If a man can become president and fool a nation into believing that he cared about the soul of a country, then I needn't feel bad about my own losses. Three hundred and sixty million Americans allowed him to be in power for four years, minus a couple hundred thousand who died from coronavirus.

I saw the same sad reality of a person in power caring about finances more than human life, while my ex filed more motions in an attempt to eliminate child support. Writing it down helped me remember my personal history and how it related to the history of the world.

Unfortunately, this would also be a historical part of women's history, because I wasn't the only woman who showed up to court with a narc, year after year. Court was a common stage for a narc. I waited for D-Day while focusing on my own self-worth.

Establish Self-Rule #7 - Write and Share Your Story (safely, privately, anonymously, always/at all times protecting your custody case. NOTE: not for the purposes of defaming an ex or character assassination.) To fully heal, we have to "purge our pain onto the page." Know the benefits of a purge in the process of transformation. We need to get out of us what's blackened us and fill in the void with light and truth. We can journal our way to clarity and out of any confusion and/or cognitive dissonance. Also, be writing down (date, time, incident) of any bad behavior of the narcissist. This can be helpful for a custody case and contempt motion. Documentation was how I went on to win my case later in my battles. Establish a documentation system. Need a Google Doc of all the false allegations? Create this. Calmly, list the lies as they get thrown at you. Number them 1-100 with date, time, claim, and evidence (screen-shots). Write your simple 1-3 sentence disclaiming the nonsense. This way you don't waste energy defending yourself to the narcissist but you start tracking their behavior to expose later.

Self-Reflection Questions:

- How could writing help you?
- Can you start a journal or commit to writing regularly to put words to your experiences?
- Can you write a letter to yourself?
- Can you write an email to yourself?
- Can you write a text or memo to record your feelings?
- Is there a friend that you could write to?
- How can you incorporate writing about your journey into your life?

Bonus: Self-Rule #8

STAGE A COMEBACK

"There is no point in lingering in feeling defeated."
—a journal entry

After spending years overreacting to the narc and playing a defensive legal strategy, I certainly knew the value of in-depth, long reflections. To change my unfavorable legal outcome, I had to take an inventory of my lengthy court history with the narc, and especially pick apart the pieces of the trial in which I lost. I needed to see and acknowledge both my strengths and my weaknesses when it came to Family Court. I needed to "own" the part of me that felt small and ill-equipped for a legal battle. I needed to take a loving look at the scared part of me that hired a low-income attorney, and kept using the same strategy of "playing nice" with the narc while hoping for a different outcome. The fact is that my "playing nice" got me in trouble, and got him out of it.

"I did the same thing over and over, year after year, and got the same results in Family Court against the narc. I need to rethink my original plan of quietly playing to get along—and now play to confront."
- a journal entry

The Danger in Complacency

I was disappointed in myself for many reasons. Regrettably, I had grown complacent in many ways. Two hundred years ago, the women's suffrage leader herself—Susan B. Anthony, warned women against complacency. After experiencing first-hand how complacency in my life resulted in great loss, I became willing to face my fears. I was being passive and fearful while small injustices kept adding up. Though easier said, than done, I needed to take an offensive stance to attain a different outcome. I needed to step up and out of my lethargy, and my comfortable seat on the sidelines, and start throwing punches. It was the only way to beat a bully.

> "I have to limit my expectations and stick to my principles!"
> —*a journal entry*

My first bold move was to hire a new attorney. Experience taught me that above all else, I needed an even match against my ex's hired help. I had hung onto my attorney because he was a good guy and took all my phone calls. He understood my financial woes and knew very well the complicated history. The years of court cost me very little by sticking to him and his strategy. In my fear and concern at that time, he seemed like my best option.

> "I have to reflect on the fact that it could have been worse!"
> —*a journal entry*

However, in truth and reflection, he was a defense-type attorney with the style of being passive and seeing what happens. He liked to "wing it to win it," but that style only got me so far, and not to where I'd hoped. I needed someone prepared, someone more experienced in Family Court, and someone more knowledgeable about my legal opponent. I had stuck with my attorney's advice and strategy, and I lost. It was a relationship that I needed to sever in order to move forward and try to gain some semblance of justice for my daughter and me. I also had to speak up to the narc on Our Family Wizard and call him on things he was doing that weren't appropriate for a child her age. Both of these changes took tremendous courage. I had to process what happened at the trial, how the narc played, and change at my core.

> "I find it interesting that the narc has nothing to say now that I say things and question his thoughts and behavior."
> —*a journal entry*

A Crisis Can be an Opportunity

> "Spiritual teachers preach that I gain more through my losses in life. I need to see what was gained here. Even if I just gained clarity that I need a new attorney."
> —*a journal entry*

My loss in Family Court felt so big and so bad that it was going to take time, skill, energy, and attention to detail to attempt any type of reversal. I have always loved the saying: "Rome wasn't built in a day!" It reminds me that all of my small steps do add up. I hung onto the fact that she was with me half of the time, and I could still be a good influence in all those moments. I'd show her a life of friends, cooperation, consistency, and academic success—all things that the narc never paid much attention to. The narc lacked so many basic human components that I instinctively knew that I had to "fill in the blanks," so to speak. All that he lacked in compassion, he made up for in money. That had always been his true advantage in court. However, money couldn't buy love, happiness, or his apparent lack of empathy which a child so desperately needs.

> **"My regret is a prison where I keep myself for something that I can't go back and fix. I don't think my regret is serving me, nor helping me move forward."**
> —*a journal entry*

A New Perspective on the Problem Person

> **"My attorney says that you can be 100% telling the truth and lose in Family Court. And also, you can be 100% lying and win in Family Court. That is the reality. What!?"**
> —*a journal entry*

Like any frantic mother, I researched online on how to fix, deal, cope, understand, beat, win, and triumph over my situation. I once watched a video on YouTube where a psychiatrist explained the thinking of some criminals in jail. I will never forget this most important insight. He said most just wanted to see what they could get away with, and most were narcs. When I realized that the narc just wanted to see how much he could get away with before being caught, I realized that I needed to make it clear he would NOT get away without consequences for his actions. To truly do this, I'd need a proactive offensive legal game going forward. I needed to prepare myself for this fundamental change in my approach. Prior to this valuable insight, I was so afraid of making the narc angry that I rarely confronted his inappropriate parenting. However, his lack of consequences became consequences of my own. I needed to change this. If he finally had to answer for his actions, then perhaps he wouldn't like playing the game so much. Perhaps it could put a stop to the nonsense. Perhaps a judge could see what he mistakenly did with his ruling. All I could do was give it a try.

> "I must follow the judge's order—even if it's not fair. "
> —*a journal entry*

Keeping Long-Term Helpful People in Place

> "Just like the ex tries to eliminate anyone who sees his mask drop, I need to keep those who know his true nature around."
> —*a journal entry*

I did discover something very interesting with the narc and his preference in people. Those who were involved with us for years could easily spot that he was the real problem in our case. Those who were new to our case were instantly fooled. This was important for me to recognize, because it meant that I needed to stick with the people who had figured it out for themselves and knew us long enough. The new people were dangerous in their ignorance of the co-parenting situation.

When I caught on to this commonality, I decided to keep my child's family therapist in place for several years. I also asked the judge to keep the supervised exchanges going, as well, for as long as possible. I made a point of keeping things in place for long periods of time—this included court. With my new realization that things needed to stay in place for him to be seen, the judge would now be one of the people who would see us year after year, and problem after problem. I needed to show the judge just WHO the problem was.

> "I need to keep some long-term people in place."
> —*a journal entry*

Picking My Battles

> "I have to resign myself to the fact that co-parenting with a narc is going to involve the courts. Lots and lots of Family Court."
> —*a journal entry*

My child was always being subjected to some type of harm by the narc. In my anger and rage, I wanted to fight it all. Initially, I did, but it wore me and my first attorney out. I had to learn to simplify and stay in the game. After watching the back-and-forth between attorneys, the legal process was certainly a game to be played. I needed a more experienced attorney to match my newly-healed self, in order to play a better game. With clear intention, I set out to choose, create, and carve a new path. Most importantly, I maintained these 8 Self-Rules as foundational principles for me going forward. Each Self-Rule mattered for me at different times. I relied on these powerful self-guidelines.

> "I need to stay in the day as much as
> I need to plan for the future."
> —*a journal entry*

Making a Come-Back

> "This is the BIG question, now:
> How am I going to live my life?"
> —*a journal entry*

Since the court was a stage, and the narc loved drama and a show, I decided to stage my own comeback. I wanted my rights rightfully returned to me. I would demand some respect. Some people say that the only failure is in quitting. I had originally come from a very disempowered place and needed to step into my empowerment to take powerful action. This is where my old story ends, and my new story begins. Meanwhile, I practiced good parenting, patience, and persistence. I went into planning mode and outlined steps that I could take in order to gain my power back. I filled my mind with positive affirmations on a daily basis. I stopped doubting myself and doubted the narc instead. I had been through so much, which validated my ability to be resilient. I prayed for healing for myself and the courage to continue. I kept fighting, pressing, looking, and leaning forward. I focused on how much I mattered to my child, not how much the narc did. Most importantly, I approved of myself, one hundred times a day. Self-approval was what I needed all along. No one else's opinion mattered, not even the misinformed, lacking-true-insight judge.

Establish Self-Rule #8 - Stage a Comeback (using careful legal planning) Know that whatever order was written that this is not the end of your story. You never stop being a parent. And you can find ways to appeal to a judge on your child's behalf. You can get creative after you establish a strong mindset and stay sane. If you fall into insanity, you weaken your case. This is why these are Self-Rule for sanity. Your sanity in the midst of insanity is your secret weapon. So, stay sane.

> "I have evolved . . . I went from how do I avoid court, because I
> am afraid of battle, to how do I use it to protect my child?"
> —*a journal entry*

Self-Reflection Questions:

- How do you envision yourself having a happy future?
- What would be a good legal outcome?
- What steps could you take towards your goals?
- What would you like to change about your current circumstance?

Letter to My Readers

> **"I am a survivor."**
> —*a journal entry*

Dear Reader,

Thank you for reading my story of survival. I truly appreciate my readers and those who have sent me testimonies and shared their similar stories. I am grateful for all of you who leave me words of affirmation, encouragement, and support to keep writing my truth. I hope you have found this book helpful—that you have found something here to use to make a positive change in your and your child's life. You are a survivor, just like me. May you always see your own strength and importance.

Due to the nature of this topic, great care must be taken to protect everyone's safety in these situations. I urge you to act with wisdom and clarity, and to have your decisions backed by legal support. If it's safe for you to do so, I encourage you to seek healing support in whatever way you possibly can. I am providing a list of additional resources that can get you started on your path to healing and help. Seek out what you need for you.

If applicable, I also advise on obtaining good legal counsel—even if you need to interview several attorneys to find one that is right for you and your situation. (Check out my Get-The-Right-Lawyer-Guide online PDF) We have many aspects of our lives to consider in our individual circumstances. In our decision-making, we have to include our current financial, emotional, and housing matters. Most importantly, we have to think about the view from our child's eyes.

Knowledge is power, so I also believe that self-education and learning about this unique dilemma can help to create a better outcome. Learn. And always remember that you can only do what you are capable of doing at the time. I had to accept this true statement and forgive myself for the past.

Please be smart, safe, and practice good self-care. Many wishes of happiness, joy, and blessings in your parenting journey. Be sure to give yourself time to process the pain, grieve the losses, learn from past mistakes, and find new footing after any setback. I had to comply with the judge's order and do all that was required. Following the order = respecting the judge.

May you and your children be well. I wish that you find happiness with your children, even if it is only in the times between the problems. I send you my love, truth, light, and support for those inevitable tough times. I am cheering you on during the painful moments. Keep being a good parent—no matter what the other parent is doing. You matter.

> **"As long as you live, keep learning how to live."**
> *—Lucius Annaeus Seneca*

May you learn how to live with whatever you are going through.
I leave you with my love.

Sincerely,

Grace W. Wioldson

Helpful Resources

National Services:

National Domestic Violence Hotline: 1-800-799-7233
https://www.thehotline.org/

National Suicide Prevention Lifeline: 1-800-273-8255
https://suicidepreventionlifeline.org/

Victims of Sexual Assault (DoD) Safe Helpline: 1-877-995-5247
https://safehelpline.org/about

Helpful Groups:

Alcoholics Anonymous:
https://www.aa.org/

Adult Children of Alcoholics and Dysfunctional Families:
https://adultchildren.org/

Al-Anon (for Friends and Family of Alcoholics):
https://al-anon.org/

Co-Dependents Anonymous:
https://coda.org/

Grace's Other Books:

Book#1- *So, You Love an Alcoholic?: Lessons for a Codependent*
https://www.amazon.com/dp/B09299JKD5

Book#2- *I Loved an Alcoholic, But Hated the Drinking: 11 Essential Strategies to Survive Codependency and Live in Recovery with Self-Love*
https://www.amazon.com/dp/B07GH5P3TD

– Grace's Co-Parenting Series –

Book#3 - *Co-Parenting with a Narcissist: 7 Self-Rules to Stay Sane (A Survivor's Story)*
https://www.amazon.com/dp/B08CBQGYR4

Book#4 - *How-To Fight a Narcissist in Family Court and Win: Super-Smart Strategies for Success*
https://www.amazon.com/dp/B08WH4VNP7

Book#5 - *Co-Parenting with a Sociopath: Survival and Sanity Guide*
https://www.amazon.com/dp/B09BWR5BDX

Coming soon!
How To Survive a Custody Battle with a Narcissist: When the Family Courts Force You to Co-Parent

Other helpful books:

BIFF Quick Responses to High-Conflict People, Their Personal Attacks, Hostile Email and Social Media Meltdowns by Bill Eddy, LCSW, Esq.

Splitting: Protecting Yourself While Divorcing Someone with Borderline or Narcissistic Personality Disorder
by Bill Eddy LCSW JD and Randi Kreger

5 Types of People Who Can Ruin Your Life: Identifying and Dealing with Narcissists, Sociopaths, and Other High-Conflict Personalities by Bill Eddy

Codepedent No More: How to Stop Controlling Others and Start Caring for Yourself by Melody Beattie

Facing Love Addiction: Giving Yourself the Power to Change the Way You Love, by Pia Mellody

Websites:

Al-Anon Family Groups (for friends and family of alcoholics)
https://al-anon.org/

Narcissist Abuse Recovery & Self-Empowerment with Melanie Tonia Evans https://www.melanietoniaevans.com/
https://www.youtube.com/user/MelanieToniaEvans

YouTube Channels:

Grace Wroldson
Melanie Tonia Evans
Rebecca Zung
DoctorRamani

Follow Me on Facebook!

Co-Parenting with a Narcissist: 7 Self-Rules to Stay Sane
@coparentingwithanarcissistcustodybattle
https://www.facebook.com/coparentingwithanarcissistcustodybattle

Facebook Groups:

Co-Parenting with a Narcissist Support Group for Moms
www.facebook.com/groups/coparentingwithanarcissistformoms/

More About the Author

Grace W. Wroldson fell in love with an alcoholic, but little did she know that a serious personality disorder was also lurking beneath the surface. Desperate to save him, she entered the rooms of recovery in the Twelve-Step Family Groups of Al-Anon, trying to find a way to help him reach sobriety in AA—or, at least, give up drinking!

She was under the influence of what she calls the "codependent spell." Too busy looking for help for him, she failed to see how desperately she needed help for herself. She was codependent and unknowingly being abused.

In her first book, ***So, You Love an Alcoholic?: Lessons for a Codependent***, Grace shares more than twenty-five incredibly valuable lessons for anyone going through the same dilemma. She shares her powerful awakenings, insights, and moments of crystal-clear clarity, leaving her readers in awe of her strength and determination to save herself.

Initially, it was just his drinking that bothered her, so she stayed in the relationship, justifying everything. She spent fifteen years trying to love a man into wholeness and happiness, only to destroy herself in the process by the effects of both of their disorders. Plagued with love addiction and trauma bonds, her codependency recovery wasn't all she was faced with. At her worst, she found herself pregnant with the alcoholic's child— abandoned, living in poverty, and emotionally defeated.

With a spiritual epiphany, Grace broke free of her addiction— her addiction to loving him—and escaped the painful relationship. She suffered torturous heartbreak and withdrawal, but she pulled through and survived. Her "codependent spell" was broken with her dedication to her codependency recovery. Then, with enough distance and healing, she broke trauma bonds.

Courageously, she then raised her child on her own. However, despite her attempts to keep her unstable ex away, the family courts forced her to share her baby with an alcoholic who refused to get better.

Determined to raise her child safely with the disease close at her heels,

Grace worked her own program of recovery even harder to raise her child in an alcohol-free home—keeping her a safe distance from the alcoholic. In her second book, *I Loved An Alcoholic But Hated the Drinking,* Grace shares eleven more of her hard-won survival strategies.

For many years, she enjoyed success and watched her child thrive—until her ex went on the attack. Being subjected to years of abuse by proxy in the family courts, her attorney realized her ex was a disordered narcissist and brought the true problem to light. To repair the new level of damage, Grace found healing programs specific to Narcissistic Abuse Syndrome. By maintaining her sanity, she was able to be the best parent that she could be, oftentimes under horrific conditions. She focused on "one day at a time," creating a happy life and fun-filled childhood for her daughter. With the **Self-Rules** she created and practiced, Grace was able to continue fighting for her and her daughter's rights—learning how to truly win the war.

Now, with twenty years of "program wisdom" and personal experience under her belt, Grace shares her secrets, strategies, and successes on how to navigate the storms of dealing with an alcoholic, narcissistic ex. in this book and her follow-up book *How-To Fight a Narcissist in Family Court and Win: Super-Smart Strategies for Success.* With her solid foundation in a recovery program (Al-Anon for friends and family of alcoholics), she was able to embrace a life of choices and turn her life around, creating her own happy ending—full of self-love.

Now, breaking her silence, she shares her message of hope, healing, and true transformation.

After losing—then winning—in family court, she went on to write another survival book; *Co-Parenting with a Sociopath: Survival and Sanity Guide* giving readers keys to survival and staying sane—while uncovering the disorders of her ex. Through the implementation of core principles, she was able to establish peace, stop the attacks, and halt the abuse. As a result, she was able to thrive, and enjoy more than half-time with her child—while her child was privileged to have many activities and therapy. Most importantly, she was able to remain in her child's life despite her ex's attempts to eliminate her.

If you resonate with Grace's story, be sure to buy a copy of her other books to learn all of her life-saving lessons and survival strategies, today!

Also Available on Amazon!

Also Available on Amazon!

Learn with Grace

Heal with Grace

Grow with Grace

Printed in Great Britain
by Amazon